cute & easy
little knits

cute & easy
little knits

35 quick and quirky projects you'll love to make

NICKI TRENCH

CICO BOOKS

LONDON NEW YORK

Published in 2017 by CICO Books
An imprint of Ryland Peters & Small Ltd

20–21 Jockey's Fields   341 E 116th St
London WC1R 4BW   New York, NY 10029

www.rylandpeters.com

10 9 8 7 6 5 4 3 2 1

A CIP catalog record for this book is available from
the Library of Congress and the British Library.

ISBN: 978 1 78249 484 3

Printed in China

Editor: Marie Clayton
Pattern checker: Jane Czaja
Designer: Luana Gobbo
Photographer: Emma Mitchell
Illustrator: Stephen Dew
Stylist: Nel Haynes

In-house editor: Anna Galkina
Head of production: Patricia Harrington
Publishing manager: Penny Craig
Publisher: Cindy Richards

contents

introduction

This book is full of the most charming little things to knit; I have thoroughly enjoyed creating the projects for you, and I hope they will be a joy to make. The items are all designed with simplicity in mind, but I hope those of you with more experience will also still enjoy making them. Those with less experience will find the Knitting basics section at the back of the book very useful.

Sometimes the simplest things are the most beautiful. There are many favorites of mine in this book, but possibly my most favorite are the Lavender pouches with their cute little bows. The Cheeky mice are also difficult to resist, as are the Sweet kittens.

All these projects make fantastic gifts, too—there's even a knitted Bow tie made using a gorgeous silk yarn, in dashing gray and yellow. The baby items make truly special gifts for newborns or toddlers, and you'll also find some lovely practical items such as the Sewing needle case, Chunky ribbed pompom hat, Place mats, Cable iPad cover, and the Laptop case.

A few of the designs have been purely selfish: I designed the Bright fingerless gloves because I love this yarn, the vibrant yellow color, and the pompoms. I have made lots of these in different colors, for too many people!

The projects have been knitted on a range of straight, circular, or double-pointed needles. I tend to use wooden knitting needles, because I find they are more forgiving on the hands—but use the needles of your choice. There is a Suppliers list at the back of the book, where you can find information on where to buy all the yarns, needles, and accessories you need to make the projects.

Sometimes colors and yarns are discontinued, or maybe you can't get hold of a particular yarn where you live. Don't be afraid to replace a yarn with another color, or use another yarn in the same weight. There is a gauge (tension) guide on nearly all of the projects —except where getting an exact measurement is not important—so use this to check the gauge (tension) in the new yarn before you begin.

I really hope you will make many of the projects in this book, and will have as much fun as I did with them.

chapter one

GIFTS FOR
LITTLE ONES

sweet kittens

Cute and simple—these are a great project for both those new and old to toy making. They take very little time, and with a little basic embroidery you can give them fun characteristics.

MATERIALS

- Debbie Bliss Baby Cashmerino, 55% wool, 33% acrylic, 12% cashmere sportweight (lightweight DK) yarn, 1¾oz (50g) balls, approx 137yd (125m) per ball: 1 x ball each of (MC): Orange shade 92 (orange) OR Clotted Cream shade 65 (cream) OR Black shade 300 (black) OR Dark Grey shade 58 (dark gray) OR Ecru shade 101 (off white) OR Candy Pink shade 06 (pink) (MC)
- US size 3 (3.25mm) straight knitting needles
- Set of US size 3 (3.25mm) double-pointed needles
- Yarn sewing needle
- Polyfiber toy stuffing
- Scraps of jade green, yellow, or blue yarn for eyes
- Scraps of pale pink yarn for noses
- Scraps of black or white yarn for whiskers

SIZE

Approx 3in (7.5cm) high x 6½in (16.5cm) around

GAUGE (TENSION)

Exact gauge (tension) is not essential for this project.

ABBREVIATIONS

k	knit
kfb	knit in front and back of next stitch
k2tog	knit 2 stitches together
p	purl
pfb	purl in front and back of next stitch
rep	repeat
RS	right side
st(s)	stitch(es)
WS	wrong side
[ ]	repeat stitches in brackets number of times stated

Kitten

Using any color and US size 3 (3.25mm) straight needles, cast on 10 sts leaving a long tail.

Row 1: K to end.
Row 2: Kfb in each st. (20 sts)
Row 3: Pfb in each st. (40 sts)
Row 4: K to end.
Row 5: P to end.
Rows 6–15: Rep Rows 4 and 5.
Row 16: [K1, k2tog] to last st, k1.
Rows 17: P to end.
Rows 18–25: Rep Rows 4 and 5.
Bind (cast) off, leaving a long tail for creating ears later.

Finishing

With WS together, and with yarn tail from cast-on edge, sew first and last st of cast-on edge together. Weave yarn through all the cast-on stitches and pull tight to close hole. Sew seam from cast-on edge to bound (cast)-off edge with the same piece of yarn (to go at the center-back of kitten).

Turn RS out and stuff Kitten with toy filling.

Keeping seam at center back, and using a separate piece of yarn (leaving yarn tail from bound (cast)-off edge for creating ears later), sew seam at top of head (open end) picking up outside loop of each stitch along seam.

Thread yarn tail left from the bound (cast)-off edge (in center top of seam) onto yarn needle, insert it through center of top of head right through Kitten and out of bottom so

it makes an indentation that creates ears. Secure yarn and sew in end.

Face

Work on front of Kitten (with seam at back).

Using green, yellow, or blue yarn, embroider eyes using French knots (see page 110).

Using pale pink yarn, embroider nose with two or three straight stitches (see page 110) just below and between the eyes.

Using black yarn, embroider two whiskers in straight stitch on each side of nose.

Tail

Using MC and set of US size 3 (3.25mm) double-pointed needles, cast on 3 sts.

*Knit to end. Do not turn. Slide stitches to the other end of the needle, keeping the working yarn to the back; rep from * until Tail measures approx 2–3in (5–7.5cm).

Sew tip of one end of Tail at bottom of back of Kitten, at seam.

Curl Tail around to front of Kitten and secure first half of tail with a few stitches.

Tip *If using mattress stitch to join the back seam, join on right side.*

hooded baby jacket

I love these double-breasted jackets on babies and toddlers. This is knitted using a yarn with a slight amount of cashmere to make it really soft. If you decide to replace the yarn, make sure the alternative is also really soft.

MATERIALS

- Debbie Bliss Baby Cashmerino, 55% wool, 33% acrylic, 12% cashmere sportweight (lightweight DK) yarn, 1¾oz (50g) balls, approx 137yd (125m) per ball: 6(7:7:8:9) balls of Pool shade 71 (blue)
- US size 3 (3.25mm) knitting needles
- US size 3 (3.25mm) circular needle
- Yarn holder
- Yarn sewing needle
- 4 buttons, approx 7/8in (23mm) diameter

GAUGE (TENSION)

25 sts x 42 rows to a 4in (10cm) square over seed (moss) stitch, using US size 3 (3.25mm) needles and Baby Cashmerino.

SPECIAL ABBREVIATION

ssk—slip slip knit decrease: slip each of next two sts from left needle to right needle knitwise, insert left needle knitwise in both sts and knit them together

ABBREVIATIONS

alt	alternate
cont	continue
dec	decrease
foll	follow(s)ing
inc	increase
k	knit
kfb	knit in front and back of next stitch
k2tog	knit 2 stitches together
p	purl
patt	pattern
rem	remain(ing)
rep	repeat
RH	right hand
RS	right side
st(s)	stitch(es)
WS	wrong side
[ ]	repeat stitches in brackets number of times stated

SIZE

To fit age in months	0–6	6–12	12–18	18–24	24–36
Actual measurements: Chest	22½in (57cm)	23in (58.5cm)	24½in (62cm)	25½in (64.5cm)	27¼in (69.5cm)
Length to shoulder	14¼in (36cm)	15¼in (38.5cm)	15¾in (40cm)	16in (41cm)	17in (43cm)
Sleeve length	7in (18cm)	8in (20.5cm)	8½in (22cm)	9in (23cm)	10in (25cm)

Back

Using US size 3 (3.25mm) straight needles, cast on 71(**73**:77:**81**:87) sts. Work 4 rows in garter st (every row knit).

Start seed (moss) st:

Row 5: K1, [p1, k1] to end.
Row 6: K1, [p1, k1] to end.
Cont in seed (moss) st as set until work measures 8¼(**9**:9½:**9¾**:10)in (21:**23**:24:**24.5**:25cm)

Shape armhole:

Bind (cast) off 3(**3**:3:**4**:5) sts at beg of next two rows. (65(**67**:71:**73**:77) sts)
Dec 1 st at each end of next and foll 4 rows and then on foll 3 alt rows. (49(**51**:55:**57**:61) sts)
Cont in seed (moss) st until armhole measures 4(**4⅛**:4¼:**4½**:5⅛)in (10:**10.5**:11:**11.5**:13cm), ending on a WS row.
Next row: Bind (cast) off 6(**6**:7:**7**:8) sts, cont in seed (moss) st until 6(**6**:6:**7**:7) sts are on RH needle, turn and patt to end.
Bind (cast) off 6(**6**:6:**7**:7) sts.
Place 25(**27**:29:**29**:31) center back sts on holder.
Rejoin yarn to rem sts with RS facing and work in seed (moss) st to end.
Next row: Bind (cast) off 6(**6**:7:**7**:8) sts, cont in seed (moss) st.
Work 1 row.
Bind (cast) off rem sts.

Left front

Using US size 3 (3.25mm) straight needles, cast on 46(**50**:53:**55**:59) sts. Work 4 rows in garter st.

Start seed (moss) st:

Row 5: K1, [p1, k1] to last 1(**1**:0:**0**:0) st, p1(**1**:0:**0**:0).
Row 6: P1(**1**:0:**0**:0), k1, [p1, k1] to end.
Cont in seed (moss) st as set until work measures 8¼(**9**:9½:**9¾**:10)in (21:**23**:24:**24.5**:25cm) ending on a WS row.

Shape armhole:

Bind (cast) off 3(**3**:3:**4**:5) sts at beg of next row. (43(**47**:50:**51**:54) sts)
Work 1 row seed (moss) st.
Dec 1 st at armhole edge of next and foll 4 rows and then on foll 3 alt rows. (35(**39**:42:**43**:46) sts)
Cont in seed (moss) st until armhole measures 2¾(**2¾**:2¾:**3¼**:3¾) in (7:**7**:7:**8**:9.5cm), ending on a WS row.

Shape neck:

Next row: Patt to last 9(**9**:9:**11**:13) sts, turn and leave these sts on holder.
Dec 1 st at neck edge on next and every row until 12(**12**:13:**14**:15) sts rem.
Cont in seed (moss) st until work measures same as Back to shoulder, ending on a WS row.
Bind (cast) off 6(**6**:7:**7**:8) sts, cont in seed (moss) st.
Work 1 row.
Bind (cast) off rem sts.

Right front

Work as for Left Front, working 2 rows less to armhole shaping.

Work buttonholes:

Buttonhole row 1: Patt 4(**5**:5:**6**:6) sts, bind (cast) off 3 sts, patt until 10(**10**:11:**11**:12) sts, bind (cast) off 3 sts, patt to end.
Buttonhole row 2: Patt as set, casting on 3 sts over each bind (cast) off.
Work 1 row seed (moss) st.
Cont to foll armhole instructions as for Left Front reversing shaping until work measures 2¾in (7cm) from Buttonhole row 1, ending on a WS row.
Work Buttonhole rows 1–2 once more.
Cont shaping and working seed (moss) st until work matches Left Front to shoulder, ending on a RS row.
Bind (cast) off 6(**6**:7:**7**:8) sts, cont in seed (moss) st.
Work 1 row.
Bind (cast) off rem sts.

Sleeves

(make 2)
Using US size 3 (3.25mm) straight needles, cast on 37(**41**:45:**45**:49) sts. Work 4 rows in garter st.

Start seed (moss) st:

Row 5: K1, [p1, k1] to end.
Row 6: K1, [p1, k1] to end.
Cont in seed (moss) st as set.
Inc 1 st at each end of 5th row and every foll 4th(**6th**:6th:**6th**:6th) row to 59(**63**:65:**71**:79) sts.
Cont in seed (moss) st until work measures 7(**8**:8½:**9**:10)in (18:**20.5**:22:**23**:25cm).
Bind (cast) off 3(**3**:3:**4**:5) sts at beg of next two rows. (53(**57**:59:**63**:69) sts)
Dec 1 st at each end of next and foll 4 alt rows. (43(**47**:49:**53**:59) sts)
Work 1 row seed (moss) st.
Bind (cast) off rem sts.

Hood

Join shoulder seams.

With RS facing using US size 3 (3.25mm) circular needle, leaving edge sts on holder, pick up and k 14(**15**:15:**16**:16) sts from Right Front neck and 2 sts from Back side neck, patt across 25(**27**:29:**29**:31) Back neck sts from holder, pick up and k 2 sts from Back side neck and 14(**15**:15:**16**:16) sts from Left Front neck leaving edge sts on holder. (57(**61**:63:**65**:67) sts).

Next row: Starting with a k st work 12(**14**:14:**15**:15) sts in seed (moss) st, kfb in next 16(**16**:17:**17**:18) sts, k1, kfb in next 16(**16**:17:**17**:18) sts, starting with a p st, work to end in seed (moss) st. (89(**93**:97:**99**:103) sts) Cont in seed (moss) st until work measures 6(**6¼**:7:**7¼**:7¾)in (15:**16**:18:**18.5**:19.5cm).

Next row: Patt 41(**43**:45:**46**:48) sts, k2tog, patt 3 sts, ssk, patt to end.

Next row: Patt 40(**42**:44:**45**:47) sts, k2tog, patt 3 sts, ssk, patt to end.

Cont to dec as set for 6 more rows. (73(**77**:81:**83**:87) sts)

Bind (cast) off all sts.

Hood edging

Fold bound (cast)-off edge of hood in half and join together.

With RS facing using US size 3 (3.25mm) circular needle, k9(**9**:9:**11**:13) from Right Front holder, pick up and k107(**111**:125:**129**:135) sts around Hood edge, k9(**9**:9:**11**:13) from Left Front holder. (125(**129**:143:**151**:161) sts)

Next row: K.

Bind (cast) off all sts.

Front edging

With RS facing using US size 3 (3.25mm) straight needles, pick up and k105(**109**:113:**117**:123) sts along Left Front.

Next row: K.

Bind (cast) off all sts.

Rep for Right Front.

Finishing

Sew side and sleeve seams.

Sew sleeves in place.

Attach buttons. Weave in ends.

baby tank top

I love tank tops on babies. This is a really simple pattern, so go on and play with colors and use as many stripes as you like—the more colorful the better!

MATERIALS

- Debbie Bliss Eco Baby, 100% cotton sportweight (lightweight DK) yarn, 1¾oz (50g) balls, approx 137yd (125m) per ball:
  2(**2**:2:**3**:3) balls of Denim shade 29 (blue) (A)
  1 x ball of Ecru shade 16 (off white)(B)
- US size 2/3 (3mm) and US size 3 (3.25mm) knitting needles
- US size 2/3 (3mm) circular needle
- Yarn holder
- Yarn sewing needle

GAUGE (TENSION)

27 sts x 33 rows to a 4in (10cm) square over stockinette (stocking) stitch, using US size 3 (3.25mm) needles and Baby Cashmerino.

SIZE

To fit age in months	0–6	**6–12**	12–18	**18–24**	24–36
Actual measurements: Chest	21½in (54.5cm)	**22½in (57cm)**	23¾in (60.5cm)	**25in (63.5cm)**	26¼in (66.5cm)
Length to shoulder	9½in (24cm)	**10½in (26.5cm)**	12¼in (31cm)	**12½in (32cm)**	13½in (34cm)

ABBREVIATIONS

alt	alternate
beg	beginning
cont	continue
dec	decrease
foll	following
k	knit
p	purl
patt	pattern
rem	remain(ing)
rep	repeat
RS	right side
st(s)	stitch(es)
st st	stockinette (stocking) stitch
[ ]	repeat stitches in brackets number of times stated

Note

A stripe is worked across the chest of the garment and you will be commencing your armhole shaping while knitting the stripe in the contrasting color.

Back

Using US size 2/3 (3mm) straight needles and A, cast on 74(**78**:82:**86**:90) sts.
Row 1 (RS): K2, [p2, k2] to end.
Row 2: P2, [k2, p2] to end.
Cont in ribbing as set for a further 10(**12**:14:**14**:16) rows.
Change to US size 3 (3.25mm) needles.
Starting with a k row, work in st st for 24 (**30**:40:**42**:42) rows.
Change to B and cont in st st for the next 14(**14**:16:**16**:18) rows to work your contrasting stripe, working armhole shaping at appropriate row.
All sizes:
Cont in st st, as set in B until 28(**32**:44:**46**:44) st st rows have been completed in total.
Shape armholes:
Bind (cast) off 3(**3**:3:**4**:4) sts at beg of next 2 rows.(68(**72**:76:**78**:82) sts)
Dec 1 st at each end of next row and 3 foll RS rows. (60(**64**:68:**70**:74) sts**)
When 38(**44**:56:**58**:60) st st rows have been completed (you have completed your stripe) change back to A.
Cont straight in st st in A until 68(**74**:88:**90**:96) st st rows have been worked in total.

Shape back neck:

Next row: Bind (cast) off 13(**14**:16:**16**:16) sts, k34(**36**:36:**38**:42), bind (cast) off rem 13(**14**:16:**16**:16) sts.

Place center sts on yarn holder.

Front

Work as Back to **.

Cont straight in st st and in B until 38(**44**:56:**58**:60) st st rows have been completed.

Change back to A.

Cont straight in st st in A until 48(**54**:66:**68**:72) st st rows have been completed.

Shape neck:

Next row: K19(**21**:22:**22**:23) sts in patt, turn and cont on these sts only for left side and shoulder.

Work 1 row.

Dec 1 st at neck edge of next and foll alt rows until 13(**14**:16:**16**:16) sts rem.

Cont straight in st st until 68(**74**:88:**90**:96) st st rows have been worked in total.

Bind (cast) off rem shoulder sts.

With RS facing, slip center 22(**22**:24:**26**:28) sts onto a holder, rejoin yarn to rem sts, k to end.

Work 1 row.

Dec 1 st at neck edge of next and foll alt rows until 13(**14**:16:**16**:16) sts rem.

Complete to match left neck and shoulder, reversing shoulder shaping.

Neckband

Join shoulder seams.

With RS facing, using US size 2/3 (3mm) circular needle and A, k34(**36**:36:**38**:42) sts from Back neck holder, pick up and k16(**17**:20:**22**:23) sts down left side of Front neck, k22(**22**:24:**26**:28) from Front neck holder, pick up and k16(**17**:20:**22**:23) sts up right side of Front neck. (88(**92**:100:**108**:116) sts)

Round 1: Working in the round, [k2, p2] to end.

Rep Round 1 a further 5 times.

Bind (cast) off in rib.

Armbands

Join side seams.

With RS facing, using US size 2/3 (3mm) circular needle and A, pick up and k60(**64**:64:**68**:76) sts evenly around armhole edge.

Round 1: Working in the round, [k2, p2] to end.

Rep Round 1 a further 5 times.

Bind (cast) off in rib. Rep around other armhole.

Finishing

Weave in ends.

baby bear beanie hat

Beanie hats with ears are always the cutest. This hat is made using a gorgeously soft Baby Cashmerino yarn from the Debbie Bliss Collection, and has cute little bear ears.

MATERIALS

- Debbie Bliss Baby Cashmerino, 55% wool, 33% acrylic, 12% cashmere sportweight (lightweight DK) yarn, 1¾oz (50g) balls, approx 137yd (125m) per ball:
  1 x ball of Silver shade 12 (pale gray)
- US size 6 (4mm) circular needle, 16in (40cm) length
- US size 4 (3.5mm) knitting needles
- Yarn sewing needle
- 8 stitch markers

SIZE

To fit age 6–24 months

FINISHED MEASUREMENT

Approx 16–18in (40.5–46cm) circumference, 6½in (16.5cm) high

GAUGE (TENSION)

21 sts x 28 rows to a 4in (10cm) square over stockinette (stocking) stitch, using US size 6 (4mm) needles and Baby Cashmerino.

SPECIAL ABBREVIATION

ssk—slip slip knit decrease: slip each of next two sts from left needle to right needle knitwise, insert left needle knitwise in both sts and knit them together

ABBREVIATIONS

approx	approximately
beg	beginning
k	knit
k2tog	knit 2 stitches together
p	purl
p2tog tbl	purl 2 stitches together through the back of the loops
rem	remain(ing)
rep	repeat
RS	right side
st st	stockinette (stocking) stitch
st(s)	stitch(es)

Hat

Using US size 6 (4mm) circular needle, cast on 80 sts. Place marker to indicate beg of round.

Work in st st (every round k from RS) until work measures approx 6in (15cm)—bottom edge of hat will roll up.

Next round: *K10, place marker; rep from * to end. (8 stitch markers)

Begin decreases:

*K to 2 sts before marker, k2tog; rep from * until there are 8 sts left on needle.

Cut yarn, thread end into yarn sewing needle, and draw through rem 8 sts.

Ears

(make four)

Using US size 4 (3.5mm) knitting needles, cast on 15 sts, leaving a long tail for sewing Ears together and sewing onto Hat later.

Row 1: K to end.

Row 2: P to end.

Rep Rows 1 and 2 until 10 rows have been worked.

Ear top:

Row 1: Ssk, k to last 2 sts, k2tog. (13 sts)

Row 2: P2tog, p to last 2 sts, p2tog tbl. (11 sts)

Row 3: Rep Row 1. (9 sts)

Row 4: Rep Row 2. (7 sts)

Bind (cast) off.

Finishing

Weave in ends.

Take two Ear pieces and place RS together. Sew around Ear with backstitch, leaving bottom open. Rep with other two Ear pieces. Pin Ears at top of Hat and sew in place.

cheeky mice

Just for the fun of it. Here is a quick and easy project for any lover of mice—perhaps even your cat!

MATERIALS

- Debbie Bliss Baby Cashmerino, 55% wool, 33% acrylic, 12% cashmere sportweight (lightweight DK) yarn, 1¾oz (50g) balls, approx 137yd (125m) per ball:
Small amount of:
Silver shade 12 (pale gray) OR Orange shade 92 (orange) OR Butter shade 83 (yellow) OR Ecru shade 101 (off white) OR Baby Blue shade 204 (pale blue) OR Apple shade 02 (green) OR Lipstick Pink shade 78 (pink) OR Peach Melba shade 68 (peach) OR Clotted Cream shade 65 (cream) OR Kingfisher shade 72 (bright green)
Black shade 300
- US size 4 (3.5mm) knitting needles
- Yarn sewing needle
- Small amount of stuffing or spare yarn ends

SIZE

Approx 2in (5cm) long

GAUGE (TENSION)

Exact gauge (tension) is not essential for this project.

ABBREVIATIONS

approx	approximately
k	knit
kfb	knit in front and back of next stitch
k2tog	knit 2 stitches together
p	purl
pfb	purl in front and back of next stitch
p2tog	purl 2 stitches together
p3tog	purl 3 stitches together
rep	repeat
RS	right side
st(s)	stitch(es)
st st	stockinette (stocking) stitch
WS	wrong side

Mouse

Using any color, cast on 3 sts, leaving a long tail.

Row 1: Kfb of first st, k1, kfb of last st. (5 sts)

Row 2: Pfb of first st, p3, pfb of last st. (7 sts)

Row 3: Kfb of first st, k5, kfb of last st. (9 sts)

Row 4: Pfb of first st, p7, pfb of last st. (11 sts)

Row 5: Kfb of first st, k9, kfb of last st. (13 sts)

Work 7 rows in st st.

Next row: K2tog, k to last 2 sts, k2tog. (11 sts)

Next row: P2tog, p to last 2 sts, p2tog. (9 sts)

Next row: K2tog, k to last 2 sts, k2tog. (7 sts)

Next row: P2tog, p to last 2 sts, p2tog. (5 sts)

Next row: K2tog, k to last 2 sts, k2tog. (3 sts)

Next row: P3tog.

Fasten off, leaving a long tail.

Finishing

With RS together, sew seam lengthwise using a long tail, leaving small gap for stuffing. Turn RS out. Stuff Mouse. Sew gap closed.

Leave other tail end sticking out for the Mouse's tail. With a pin or needle divide the strands out on the tail.

Using black yarn, embroider a small nose and eyes. With same color yarn as Mouse, embroider two loops for each ear.

baby stroller blanket

This is so pretty, contemporary, and the perfect size for a stroller or car seat. It's made using a lovely chevron stripe pattern, with cute pompoms on the edges.

MATERIALS

- Debbie Bliss Rialto DK, 100% merino wool light worsted (DK) yarn, 1¾oz (50g) balls, approx 115yd (105m) per ball:
  2 x balls each of:
  Citrus shade 69 (yellow) (A)
  Duck Egg shade 19 (pale blue) (B)
  Coral shade 55 (coral) (C)
  Ecru shade 02 (off white) (D)
- US size 6 (4mm) knitting needles
- Yarn sewing needle

SIZE

Approx 27 x 19½in (69 x 49cm)

GAUGE (TENSION)

Approx 24 sts x 30 rows to a 4in (10cm) square over pattern, using US size 6 (4mm) needles and Rialto DK.

ABBREVIATIONS

approx	approximately
k	knit
kfb	knit in front and back of next stitch
k2tog	knit 2 stitches together
p	purl
rep	repeat
RS	right side
st(s)	stitch(es)
WS	wrong side

SPECIAL ABBREVIATION

ssk—slip slip knit decrease: slip each of next two sts from left needle to right needle knitwise, insert left needle knitwise in both sts and knit them together

Blanket

Using A, cast on 128 sts.
Row 1: P to end.
Row 2: K1, kfb, k4, ssk, k2tog, k4, *kfb in each of next 2 sts, k4, ssk, k2tog, k4; rep from * to last 2 sts, kfb in next st, k1.
Row 3: Rep Row 1.
Cut A, join B.
Row 4: Rep Row 2.
Row 5: Rep Row 1.
Row 6: Rep Row 2.
Cut B, join C.
Row 7: Rep Row 1.
Row 8: Rep Row 2.
Row 9: Rep Row 1.
Cut C, join D.
Row 10: Rep Row 2.
Row 11: Rep Row 1.
Row 12: Rep Row 2.
Cut D, join A.
Rep Rows 1–12 until Blanket measures approx 26½in (66.5cm), ending on a Row 12.
Rep Rows 1–3 once more.
Bind (cast) off.

Finishing

Weave in ends.
  Make a small pompom (see page 109) in each color and attach one pompom in each corner of the Blanket.

little squares blanket

I designed this blanket originally to be used as a crib blanket—but it's so pretty that it's suitable as a cozy couch blanket, too. The colors are lovely, but feel free to mix and match to your own color scheme.

MATERIALS

- Debbie Bliss Baby Cashmerino, 55% wool, 33% acrylic, 12% cashmere sportweight (lightweight DK) yarn, 1¾oz (50g) balls, approx 137yd (125m) per ball:
  5 x balls of Ecru shade 101 (off white) (A)
  3 x balls each of:
  Rose Pink shade 94 (pink) (B)
  Apple shade 02 (green) (C)
  Light Blue shade 202 (pale blue) (D)
  Mallard shade 59 (dark blue) (E)
  Silver shade 12 (pale gray) (F)
  Lipstick Pink shade 78 (bright pink) (G)
  Amber shade 66 (yellow) (H)
- US size 3 (3.25mm) knitting needles
- US size 3 (3.25mm) circular needle
- Yarn sewing needle

SIZE

45½ x 51in (116 x 130cm), including ¾in (2cm) border

GAUGE (TENSION)

Each square measures approx 2¾in (7cm) square, using US size 3 (3.25mm) knitting needles and Baby Cashmerino.

ABBREVIATIONS

alt	alternate
approx	approximately
inc	increasing
k	knit
rep	repeat
RS	right side
st(s)	stitch(es)

SPECIAL ABBREVIATIONS

sl1p—slip 1 stitch purlwise with yarn in front
s2togkpo—with yarn at back, slip 2 stitches together knitwise, knit 1, pass 2 slipped stitches over
k1tbl—knit 1 stitch through the back loop

COLORWAY

Make a total of 288 squares:
55 squares in A.
35 squares in B.
36 squares in C.
36 squares in D.
24 squares in E.
36 squares in F.
36 squares in G.
30 squares in H.

Square

Using US size 3 (3.25mm) straight needles, cast on 31 sts.

Row 1: K to end.

Row 2: Sl1p, k13, s2togkpo, k13, k1tbl. (29 sts)

Row 3 and all alt rows: Sl1p, knit to last st, k1tbl.

Row 4: Sl1p, k12, s2togkpo, k12, k1tbl. (27 sts)

Row 6: Sl1p, k11, s2togkpo, k11, k1tbl. (25 sts)

Row 8: Sl1p, k10, s2togkpo, k10, k1tbl. (23 sts)

Row 10: Sl1p, k9, s2togkpo, k9, k1tbl. (21 sts)

Row 12: Sl1p, k8, s2togkpo, k8, k1tbl. (19 sts)

Row 14: Sl1p, k7, s2togkpo, k7, k1tbl. (17 sts)

Row 16: Sl1p, k6, s2togkpo, k6, k1tbl. (15 sts)

Row 18: Sl1p, k5, s2togkpo, k5, k1tbl. (13 sts)

Row 20: Sl1p, k4, s2togkpo, k4, k1tbl. (11 sts)

Row 22: Sl1p, k3, s2togkpo, k3, k1tbl. (9 sts)

Row 24: Sl1p, k2, s2togkpo, k2, k1tbl. (7 sts)

Row 26: Sl1p, k1, s2togkpo, k1, k1tbl. (5 sts)

Row 28: Sl1p, s2togkpo, k1tbl. (3 sts)

Row 30: S2togkpo.

Cut yarn and pull through last stitch to fasten off.

Finishing

Lay squares out RS up on a flat surface with colors randomly placed, with 16 squares across x 18 squares down. With RS together, sew the squares together in strips using whipstitch (see page 108) and one of the colors from each pair of squares, to disguise the stitching.

Press the seams lightly using a damp cloth.

Border

Using A and US size 3 (3.25mm) circular needle, and with RS facing, pick up and k 240 sts along top edge. (15 sts along each square)

K 8 rows, inc 1 st at each end of all RS rows.

Bind (cast) off.

Pick up and k 240 sts along bottom edge.

K 8 rows, inc 1 st at each end of all RS rows.

Bind (cast) off.

Pick up and k 270 sts along one side edge.

Knit 8 rows, inc 1 st at each end of all RS rows.

Bind (cast) off.

Pick up and k 270 sts along second side edge.

Knit 8 rows, inc 1 st at each end of all RS rows.

Bind (cast) off.

With RS together, sew border seams at the corners.

star and pompom garland

I think this would work really well in a baby or child□s room. But it's so pretty, it's tempting to hang it anywhere around the house!

MATERIALS

- Debbie Bliss Rialto DK, 100% merino wool light worsted (DK) yarn, 1¾oz (50g) balls, approx 115yd (105m) per ball:
  1 x ball each of:
  Fuchsia shade 34 (bright pink)
  Vintage Pink shade 66 (pale pink)
  Plum shade 61 (purple)
  Mallard shade 82 (teal blue)
  Ecru shade 02 (off white)
  Willow shade 59 (pale green)
  Lake shade 86 (dark blue)
  Citrus shade 69 (bright yellow)
  Banana shade 57 (pale yellow)
- US size 6 (4mm) double-pointed needles

SIZE

Approx 78in (195cm) long

GAUGE (TENSION)

Exact gauge (tension) is not essential for this project.

ABBREVIATIONS

approx	approximately
beg	begin
k	knit
k2tog	knit 2 stitches together
kfb	knit in front and back of next stitch
p	purl
p2tog	purl 2 stitches together
rep	repeat
st(s)	stitch(es)
WS	wrong side
[ ]	repeat stitches in brackets number of times stated

SPECIAL ABBREVIATION

s1, k1, psso—slip 1 stitch, knit 1 stitch, pass slipped stitch over

Stars

(make 18—2 in each color)

Cast on 5 sts, divide sts onto
3 needles, and join in the round.

Round 1: [Kfb] around. (10 sts)

Round 2: K to end.

Round 3: [Kfb] around. (20 sts)

Round 4: K to end.

Round 5: *[Kfb] twice, k2; rep from *
to end. (30 sts)

Round 6: K to end.

Round 7: *[Kfb] twice, k4, kfb; rep
from * to end. (40 sts)

Round 8: K to end.

Round 9: *[Kfb] twice, k6, kfb; rep
from * to end. (50 sts)

Round 10: K to end.

***Beg working in rows for star
points:***

Row 11: K10, turn.

Row 12: P10, turn.

Row 13: S1, k1, psso, k6, k2tog,
turn.

Row 14: P8, turn.

Row 15: S1, k1, psso, k4, k2tog,
turn.

Row 16: P6, turn.

Row 17: S1, k1, psso, k2, k2tog,
turn.

Row 18: P4, turn.

Row 19: S1, k1, psso, k2tog.

Row 20: P2tog, cut yarn and fasten
off, leaving 6in (15cm) tail.

Leaving 6in (15cm) tail, join yarn
where you left off on main portion
of star.

Rep Rows 11–20 for each point.

Pompoms

(make 9—1 in each color)

Make pompoms (see page 108)
approx 2in (5cm) diameter, leaving
long tail for attaching to icord.

Icord

Using two US size 6 (4mm) double-
pointed needles and Fuchsia, cast
on 3 sts. *Knit to end. Do not turn.
Slide sts to other end of needle,
keeping working yarn to back; rep
from * until work measures approx
78in (195cm).

K3tog, and fasten off.

Finishing

Sew pair of Stars in same color with
WS together.

Block and press Stars.

Lay icord length out and, leaving
approx 7–8in (17.5–20cm) free at
each end, evenly space alternating
stars and pompoms along the length
approx 4in (10cm) apart. Using
matching yarn, sew stars and
pompoms onto the icord to secure.
The drop of the yarn on the
pompoms is approx 2½in (6.5cm).

chapter two

TRENDY CASES
& BAGS

phone cover

I can't resist a phone cover. My phone screen is constantly getting scratched, so these lovely knitted covers in a simple seed (moss) stitch are the perfect protection. A great project for a beginner.

SIZE

3 x 5½in (8 x 14cm)

GAUGE (TENSION)

28 sts x 48 rows to a 4in (10cm) square over seed (moss) stitch, using US size 2/3 (3mm) needles and Scrumptious 4ply.

ABBREVIATIONS

k	knit
k2tog	knit 2 stitches together
LH	left hand
p	purl
rem	remain(ing)
rep	repeat
RH	right hand
RS	right side
st(s)	stitch(es)
WS	wrong side
[ ]	repeat stitches in brackets number of times stated

MATERIALS

- Fyberspates Scrumptious 4ply, 55% merino wool, 45% silk fingering (4ply) yarn, 3½oz (100g) skeins, approx 399yd (365m) per skein:
  1 x skein of:
  Glisten shade 318 (gray), OR Denim shade 317 (blue), OR Flying Saucer shade 311 (green)
- US size 2/3 (3mm) knitting needles
- Two pieces of fabric, each approx 3½ x 6in (9 x 15cm)
- Sewing needle and thread to match fabric

Phone cover

Using any color, cast on 22 sts.
Row 1: *K1, p1; rep from * to end.
Row 2: *P1, k1; rep from * to end.
Rows 1 and 2 form seed (moss) st, rep them until work measures 11in (28cm) or to the top of phone when knitted piece is folded in half.
Do not bind (cast) off.

Picot edging first edge:
(RS) Bind (cast) off 2 sts, *slip rem st on RH needle onto LH needle**, cast on 2 sts, bind (cast) off 4 sts; rep from * ending last rep at **, slip rem st on RH needle onto LH needle (2 sts), k2tog. Fasten off last st. (9 picots)

Picot edging second edge:
On WS of work, pick up 22 sts, rep picot edging as for first edge.

Finishing

Make lining to fit inside Cover (see page 110). Insert lining into Cover with WS of lining facing WS of Cover. Stitch in place with sewing needle and matching thread along top just underneath picot edging.

laptop case

I carry my laptop with me everywhere—and even if it goes in my suitcase, I still put it inside a knitted cover for extra protection and style.

MATERIALS

• Debbie Bliss Cashmerino Aran, 55% merino wool, 33% acrylic, 12% cashmere worsted (Aran) yarn, 1¾oz (50g) balls, approx 98yd (90m) per ball:
  1 x ball each of:
  Copper shade 80 (orange) (A)
  Stone shade 27 (pale gray) (B)
• Debbie Bliss Falkland Aran, 100% wool worsted (Aran) yarn, 3½oz (100g) balls, approx 197yd (180m) per ball:
  1 x ball of Mustard shade 07 (yellow) (C)
• US size 8 (5mm) knitting needles
• Approx 14 x 18½in (35 x 47cm) piece of fabric for lining
• Approx 40in (1m) of ribbon
• Batting (wadding) (optional)

SIZE

9in high x 13in wide (23 x 33cm)

GAUGE (TENSION)

18 sts x 24 rows to a 4in (10cm) square over stockinette (stocking) stitch, using US size 8 (5mm) needles and Cashmerino Aran.

NOTE

This cover is to fit an 11in (28cm) Macbook Air. If you are making the cover to fit a different size laptop, work out from the gauge (tension) how many stitches are required for the width. Then divide the length measurement in three, and knit colors A and C to this depth and color B to double this depth, plus an extra 2 rows for the thickness of the laptop at the bottom.

ABBREVIATIONS

k	knit
p	purl
rep	repeat
RS	right side
st(s)	stitch(es)
st st	stockinette (stocking) stitch

Laptop case

Using A, cast on 63 sts.
Row 1: K to end.
Row 2: P to end.
Rep Rows 1 and 2 eight more times.
Fasten off A and join B.
Rep Rows 1 and 2 nine times.
Fasten off B and join C.
Rep Rows 1 and 2 twenty times.
Fasten off C and join B.
Rep Rows 1 and 2 nine times.
Fasten off B and join A.
Rep Rows 1 and 2 nine times.
Bind (cast) off.

Finishing

Block and press very lightly.
Fold knitted piece in half with RS facing and cast-on and bound (cast)-off edges together. Sew side seams.

Make and insert lining following the instructions on page 110. Attach edging ribbon at top edge of the lining before slipstitching knitted piece and lining together.

Optional: For extra padding, insert batting (wadding) between lining and knitted piece.

sewing needle case

I have made so many of these and given them as gifts. A really lovely little project to make, using a pretty textured stitch.

MATERIALS

- Rowan Cotton Glace, 100% cotton light worsted (DK) yarn, 1¾oz (50g) balls, approx 125yd (115m) per ball: 1 x ball of Heather shade 828 (dark purple)
- US size 3 (3.25mm) knitting needles
- Piece of green felt for lining
- Piece of white felt or batting (wadding) for "pages"
- Pinking shears (optional)
- Scraps of fabric for decoration
- Sewing needle and green and orange thread
- Approx 10in (25.5cm) of ribbon

SIZE

Approx 3½ x 4½in (9 x 11.5cm)

GAUGE (TENSION)

Exact gauge (tension) is not essential for this project.

ABBREVIATIONS

approx	approximately
k	knit
p	purl
rep	repeat
RS	right side
st(s)	stitch(es)
WS	wrong side
[ ]	repeat stitches in brackets number of times stated, also to group sequence of stitches

Case

Cast on 45 sts.

Row 1: K1, *p3 [k1, p1] twice, k1, p5, k1, [p1, k1] twice, p3, k1; rep from * to end.

Row 2: P2, k3, [p1, k1] twice, p1, k3, p1, [k1, p1] twice, k3, p3, k3, [p1, k1] twice, p1, k3, p1, [k1, p1] twice, k3, p2.

Row 3: K3, p3, [k1, p1] 5 times, k1, p3, k5, p3, [k1, p1] 5 times, k1, p3, k3.

Row 4: K1, *p3, k3, [p1, k1] 4 times, p1, k3, p3, k1; rep from * to end.

Row 5: P2, k3, p3, [k1, p1] 3 times, k1, [p3, k3] twice, p3, [k1, p1] 3 times, k1, p3, k3, p2.

Row 6: K3, p3, k3, [p1, k1] twice, p1, k3, p3, k5, p3, k3, [p1, k1] twice, p1, k3, p3, k3.

Row 7: K1, *[p3, k3, p3], [k1, p1, k1], [p3, k3, p3], k1; rep from * to end.

Row 8: K1, *[p1, k3, p3, k3] twice, p1, k1; rep from * to end.

Row 9: K1, *[p1, k1], [p3, k3], p5, [k3, p3], [k1, p1], k1; rep from * to end.

Row 10: K1, *p1, k1, p1, [k3, p3] twice, k3, [p1, k1] twice; rep from * to end.

Row 11: K1, [p1, k1] twice, [p3, k3], p1, [k3, p3], [k1, p1] 4 times, k1, [p3, k3], p1, [k3, p3], [k1, p1] twice, k1.

Row 12: K1, [p1, k1] twice, p1, k3, p5, k3, [p1, k1] 5 times, p1, k3, p5, k3, [p1, k1] 3 times.

Row 13: P2, [k1, p1] twice, k1, p3, k3, p3, [k1, p1] twice, k1, p3, [k1, p1] twice, k1, p3, k3, p3, [k1, p1] twice, k1, p2.

Row 14: K3, [p1, k1] twice, [p1, k3] twice, [p1, k1] twice, p1, k5, [p1, k1] twice, [p1, k3] twice, [p1, k1] twice, p1, k3.
Rep Rows 1–14 twice more.
Bind (cast) off.

Finishing

Block and lightly press piece.

Cut piece of green felt slightly smaller than knitted piece. Hand sew green felt onto WS of knitted piece, using green thread.

Cut piece of white felt or batting (wadding) approx 6 x 3¼in (15 x 8cm)—with pinking shears if you have them. Lay across center of green felt (inside) and place one or two pins at outer edges. Fold whole piece in half so short ends are together, and use sewing needle and matching yarn to sew backstitch or running stitch approx ¼in (0.5cm) in along folded edge to create "spine."

Cut two pieces of fabric and sew onto inside front and back of needle case with small stitches using a needle and orange thread and a decorative stitch, such as blanket stitch (see page 110).

Cut two lengths of ribbon and position one piece at center of front and one piece at center of back edges and sew in place.

- Debbie Bliss Rialto DK, 100% merino wool DK (light worsted) yarn, 1¾oz (50g) balls, approx 115yd (105m) per ball:
  3 x balls of Citrus shade 69 (yellow)
- US size 6 (4mm) knitting needles
- 2 pieces of fabric each approx 15½ x 14¾in (39.5 x 37.5cm) for lining
- Snap fastener
- Leather bag handles

SIZE

Approx 13in (33cm) wide x 11in (30cm) high

GAUGE (TENSION)

Approx 22 sts x 31 rows to a 4in (10cm) square over Diamond Brocade stitch, using US size 6 (4mm) needles and Rialto DK.

ABBREVIATIONS

approx	approximately
k	knit
p	purl
rep	repeat
RS	right side
st(s)	stitch(es)

tote bag

I really love this bag; the textured stitch is really pretty and the lining and leather handles reinforce the knitted fabric to make it strong.

Bag

(make 2 the same)
Cast on 73 sts.
Row 1 (RS): K4, *p1, k7; rep from * to last 5 sts, p1, k4.
Row 2: P3, *k1, p1, k1, p5; rep from * to last 6 sts, k1, p1, k1, p3.
Row 3: K2, *p1, k3, rep from * to last 3 sts, p1, k2.
Row 4: P1, *k1, p5, k1, p1; rep from * to end.
Row 5: *P1, k7; rep from * to last st, p1.
Row 6: Rep Row 4.
Row 7: Rep Row 3.
Row 8: Rep Row 2.
Rep these 8 rows 11 times, or until work measures approx 10in (25.5cm), ending on a Row 8.
Do not bind (cast) off.
Seed (moss) stitch top border:
Next row: P1, k1 to end.
Rep this row 7 times more.
Bind (cast) off, break off yarn.

Finishing

Pin and block two sides of Bag.

With RS of Bag together, sew side and bottom seams. Turn RS out.

Make lining following instructions on page 110.

Sew snap fastener to inside lining of Bag.

Sew on leather handles.

Fair Isle pincushions

Fair Isle is one life's greatest pleasures. If you're new to it, try these lovely pincushions.

MATERIALS

- Debbie Bliss Baby Cashmerino, 55% wool, 33% acrylic, 12% cashmere sportweight (lightweight DK) yarn, 1¾oz (50g) balls, approx 137yd (125m) per ball:

PINCUSHION 1
1 x ball each of:
Silver shade 12 (light gray) (A)
Lipstick Pink shade 78 (pink) (B)
Mallard shade 59 (blue) (C)
Apple shade 02 (green) (D)
Acid Yellow shade 91 (yellow) (E)

PINCUSHION 2
1 x ball each of:
Apple shade 02 (green) (A)
Acid Yellow shade 91 (yellow) (B)
Lipstick Pink shade 78 (pink) (C)
Mallard shade 59 (blue) (D)
Silver shade 12 (light gray) (E)

- US size 3 (3.25mm) knitting needles
- Yarn sewing needle
- Approx 4¼ x 8½in (11 x 22cm) piece of fabric for each inner pillow
- Sewing needle and matching thread
- Polyfiber filling

SIZE

Approx 3¾in (9.5cm) square (before stuffing)

GAUGE (TENSION)

Exact gauge (tension) is not essential for this project.

ABBREVIATIONS

approx	approximately
k	knit
p	purl
rep	repeat
RS	right side
st(s)	stitch(es)
st st	stockinette (stocking) stitch

CHARTS

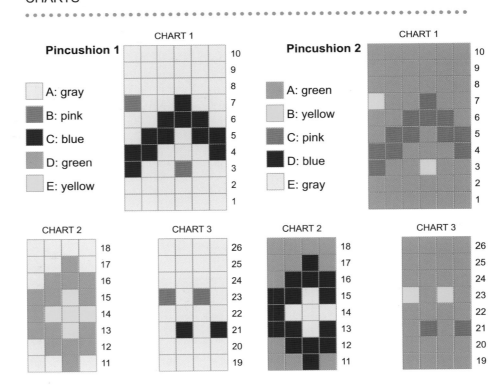

Pincushion 1

CHART 1

A: gray
B: pink
C: blue
D: green
E: yellow

CHART 2   CHART 3

Pincushion 2

CHART 1

A: green
B: yellow
C: pink
D: blue
E: gray

CHART 2   CHART 3

Pincushion front

Depending on which pincushion you want to make, refer to the colors specified in the materials list for each one and refer to the relevant charts on the left. Using A, cast on 24 sts. Working in st st, follow Charts 1, 2, and 3 to end.

Bind (cast) off.

Sew in ends.

Pincushion back

Using A, cast on 24 sts.

Row 1: K to end.

Row 2: P to end.

Rep Rows 1 and 2 (st st) until 26 rows have been worked.

Bind (cast) off.

Finishing

Pin and block Front and Back.

With RS facing, sew three seams of Front and Back together.

Make fabric pillow to fit knitted piece, and stuff with polyfiber stuffing or spare scraps of yarn.

Insert fabric pillow into knitted pocket, sew fourth seam using mattress stitch (see page 107).

bobble stitch purse

This purse is the same as the one I use all the time for my notes and coins. I also have different color versions for my make-up and jewelry when I'm traveling.

MATERIALS

- Debbie Bliss Rialto DK, 100% merino wool light worsted (DK) yarn, 1¾oz (50g) balls, approx 115yd (105m) per ball:
  1 x ball of:
  Pool shade 70 (blue) OR Jade shade 71 (green)
- US size 6 (4mm) knitting needles
- Yarn sewing needle
- Approx 7½ x 10in (20 x 26cm) piece of fabric lining
- Sewing needle and matching thread
- 6in (15cm) yellow closed-end zipper

SIZE

7 x 4½in (18 x 11.5cm)

GAUGE (TENSION)

11 bobble sts x 14 bobble rows to a 4in (10cm) square over pattern, using US size 6 (4mm) needles and Rialto DK.

ABBREVIATIONS

k	knit
LH	left hand
p	purl
rep	repeat
RH	right hand
RS	right side
st(s)	stitch(es)
yo	yarn over
yrn	yarn round needle

SPECIAL ABBREVIATION

bobble—make a bobble: start to knit next st, but do not slide st off needle, yo (to front), insert needle in st again knitwise, yrn and knit st, but do not slide st off needle, yo (to front), insert needle in st again knitwise, yrn and knit st, slide st off needle to finish st (5 sts). Turn work, yo (to back), knit these 5 stitches. Turn work, yo (to back), knit next two sts tog, slip this knitted st from RH needle onto LH needle, slip each of next three sts over knitted st separately, knit this st o complete bobble

Coin purse

Cast on 37 sts.
Row 1: K to end.
Row 2: P to end.
Row 3: K2, bobble in next st, *k3, bobble in next st: rep from * to last 2 sts, k2.
Row 4: P to end.
Row 5: K4, bobble in next st, *k3, bobble in next st; rep from * to last 4 sts, k4.
Row 6: P to end.
Rep Rows 3–6 until 30 bobble rows have been worked or work measures approx 9in (23cm).
Next row: P to end.
Bind (cast) off.

Finishing

Sew in ends. With RS together, fold in half so that the cast-on and bound (cast)-off edges meet, sew side seams. Turn RS out.

Make up lining as described on page 111. With WS facing sew zipper onto lining, and then insert lining into knitted purse and sew top edges of knitted purse on either side of zipper teeth.

cable iPad cover

It's very difficult to find little knitted projects for boys and men. I think this is a good neutral-colored project and makes a great gift.

MATERIALS

• Debbie Bliss Donegal Luxury Tweed Aran, 90% wool, 10% angora worsted (Aran) yarn, 1¾oz (50g) balls, approx 96yd (88m) per ball:
2 x balls of Pebble shade 42 (gray) (MC)
1 x ball of Tangerine shade 37 (orange) (A)
• US size 8 (5mm) straight knitting needles
• Cable needle
• Set of US size 6 (4mm) double-pointed needles
• Yarn sewing needle

SIZE

Approx 11¼ x 8in (28 x 20cm) after blocking and pressing

GAUGE (TENSION)

18 sts x 24 rows to a 4in (10cm) square over stockinette (stocking) stitch, using US size 8 (5mm) needles and Donegal Luxury Tweed Aran.

ABBREVIATIONS

approx	approximately
k	knit
LH	left hand
rep	repeat
RS	right side
st(s)	stitch(es)

SPECIAL ABBREVIATION

C4B—cable 4 back: slip next 4 sts onto cable needle and hold them behind the work. Purl next 4 sts, then transfer sts from cable needle back onto LH needle and purl these 4 sts

Cover

Using US size 8 (5mm) straight
needles and MC, cast on 56 sts.
Row 1: K8, *p8, k8; rep from * to
end.
Row 2: P8, *k8, p8; rep from * to
end.
Rep last 2 rows until 8 rows have
been worked.
Row 9: K8, *C4B, k8; rep from * to
end.
Row 10: P8, *k8, p8; rep from * to
end.
Rep last 10 rows ending with Row 4,
or until work measures approx
16in (40cm).
Bind (cast) off.

Finishing

Fold Cover over with RS together,
bringing top and bottom edges to
meet at center back. Sew the center
seam, then sew one short edge,
which will be the bottom of the cover.
Turn RS out. Block and press.

Edging

Using US size 6 (4mm) double-
pointed needles and A, starting at
seam and on RS of work, pick up
58 sts around top edge.
K 2 rounds.
Bind (cast) off.

Make and insert lining following the
instructions on page 110.

beaded purse

A pretty beaded bag for make-up or coins—I've lined it with vintage pale pink silk velvet and attached a beaded key chain, for an extra bit of glamour.

MATERIALS

- Debbie Bliss Baby Cashmerino, 55% wool, 33% acrylic, 12% cashmere sportweight (lightweight DK) yarn, 1¾oz (50g) balls, approx 137yd (125m) per ball:
  1 x ball each of:
  Chocolate shade 11 (brown) (A)
  Amber shade 66 (yellow) (B)
  Baby Blue shade 204 (pale blue) (C)
  Ecru shade 101 (off white) (D)
  Lipstick Pink shade 78 (bright pink) (E)
  Baby Pink shade 601 (pale pink) (F)
  Teal shade 203 (dark blue) (G)
  Silver shade 12 (gray) (H)
- US size 4 (3.5mm) knitting needles
- Yarn sewing needle
- 102 white seed beads size 6
- Approx 10 x 14in (25 x 35cm) piece of velvet lining fabric
- Sewing needle and matching thread
- 6in (15cm) blue closed-end zipper

SIZE

Approx 4 x 6in (10 x 15cm)

GAUGE (TENSION)

23 sts x 39 rows to a 4in (10cm) square over stockinette (stocking) stitch and garter stitch pattern, using US size 4 (3.5mm) needles and Baby Cashmerino.

ABBREVIATIONS

approx	approximately
cont	continue
k	knit
p	purl
rep	repeat
RS	right side
st(s)	stitch(es)
st st	stockinette (stocking) stitch
WS	wrong side

SPECIAL ABBREVIATION

P1B—place one bead purlwise (on RS of work)

Beaded purse

Using A, cast on 35 sts.
Garter st rows:
Row 1 (RS): K to end.
Rows 2–6: K to end.
St st rows:
Thread 17 beads onto B.
Row 7 (RS): Join B, p1, *P1B, p1;
rep from * to end.
Cont in B without beading:
Row 8 (WS): P to end.
Row 9 (RS): K to end.
Row 10 (WS): P to end.
Row 11 (RS): K to end.
Row 12 (WS): P to end.
Cut B.
Garter st rows:
Join C.
Next 6 rows: K to end.
Cut C.

St st rows:
Thread 17 beads onto D.
Next row (RS): Join D, rep Row 7.
Cont in D without beading:
Next 5 rows: Rep Rows 8–12.
Cut D.
Garter st rows:
Join E.
Next 6 rows: K to end.
Cut E.
St st rows:
Thread 17 beads onto D.
Next row (RS): Join D, rep Row 7.
Cont in D without beading:
Next 5 rows: Rep Rows 8–12.
Cut D.
Garter st rows:
Join F.
Next 6 rows: K to end.
Cut F.
St st rows:
Thread 17 beads onto G.
Next row (RS): Join G, rep Row 7.
Cont in G without beading:
Next 5 rows: Rep Rows 8–12.
Cut G.
Garter st rows:
Join H.
Next 6 rows: K to end.
Cut H.
St st rows:
Thread 17 beads onto D.
Next row (RS): Join D, rep Row 7.
Cont in D without beading:
Next 5 rows: Rep Rows 8–12.
Cut D.
Garter st rows:
Join B.
Next 6 rows: K to end.
Cut B.

St st rows:
Thread 17 beads onto H.
Next row (RS): Join H, rep Row 7.
Cont in H without beading:
Next 5 rows: Rep Rows 8–12.
Cut H.
Top border garter st rows:
Join A.
Next 6 rows: K to end.
Bind (cast) off.

Finishing

With RS together, join side seams.
Turn RS out.
Make up lining as described on
page 111. With WS facing sew zipper
onto lining, and then insert lining
into knitted purse and sew top edges
of knitted purse on either side of
zipper teeth.

chunky pompom bag

This was inspired by all those lovely vintage tapestry bags. The pompoms give it some extra glam and it's lined in a lovely velvet. The pompoms are great for using up your yarn stash.

MATERIALS

BAG
- Noro Hakone, 100% wool bulky (chunky) yarn, 3½oz (100g) skeins, approx 109yd (100m) per skein:
3 x skeins of Victorian Memoir shade 10

POMPOMS
- Debbie Bliss Rialto DK, 100% merino wool light worsted (DK) yarn, 1¾oz (50g) balls, approx 115yd (105m) per ball:
1 x ball (or small amount) each of:
Pool shade 70 (turquoise blue)
Lilac shade 85 (mauve)
Rose shade 76 (pink)
Citrus shade 69 (yellow)
Coral shade 55 (orange)
Aqua shade 44 (light blue)
Apple shade 09 (green)
- US size 10½ (6.5mm) and US size 10½/11 (7mm) knitting needles
- Yarn sewing needle
- Approx 25 x 36in (83 x 64cm) of velvet lining fabric
- Pair of round bamboo handles

SIZE

Approx 16in (40cm) wide x 10in (25cm) deep

GAUGE (TENSION)

Approx 13 sts x 20 rows to a 4in (10cm) square over seed (moss) stitch, using US size 10½/11 (7mm) needles and Noro Hakone.

ABBREVIATIONS

approx	approximately
cont	continue
k	knit
p	purl
rep	repeat
RS	right side
st(s)	stitch(es)
WS	wrong side
[ ]	repeat stitches in brackets number of times stated

Bag

Using US size 10½ (6.5mm) needles, cast on 25 sts.
Row 1: K1, [p1, k1] to end.
Row 2: P1, [k1, p1] to end.
Rep Rows 1 and 2 twice more.
Row 7: Cast on 11 sts, starting with p1, rib to end. (36 sts)
Row 8: Cast on 11 sts, starting with k1, rib to end. (47 sts)
Cont in rib as set for 4 more rows.
Change to US size 10½/11 (7mm) needles and start seed (moss) st section.
Row 13: K1, [p1, k1] to end.
Rep Row 13 until seed (moss) st section measures 21¼in (54cm).
Change to US size 10½ (6.5mm) needles and start rib section.
Row 1: P1, [k1, p1] to end.
Row 2: K1, [p1, k1] to end.
Work three more rows in rib as set.
Row 6: Bind (cast) off 11 sts in rib, rib to end. (36 sts)
Row 7: Bind (cast) off 11 sts in rib, rib to end. (25 sts)
Work five more rows in rib as set.
Bind (cast) off in rib.

Finishing

Make a lining following the instructions on page 110. Place the lining with WS together onto one half of Bag piece and hand sew in place at the side and bottom edges, making sure the stitches don't show on the right side.

Fold top ribbing part of Bag over a bamboo handle to WS at each end and sew in place.

Fold Bag over with RS together, and sew side seams. Turn RS out.

Pompoms

Make a total of 12 pompoms (see page 108) in different colors. Attach 3 in the center of the bag on each side, at the top along the bottom edge of the ribbing. Attach 3 pompoms at the top of each side seam.

chapter three

CUTE ACCESSORIES

· ·

- Mrs Moon Plump Superchunky, 80% superfine merino, 20% baby alpaca superbulky (superchunky) yarn, 3½oz (100g) skeins, approx 76yd (70m) per skein:
  1 x skein each of:
  Lemon Curd (yellow) (MC)
  Raspberry Ripple (dark pink) (A)
- Set of US size 8 (5mm) double-pointed needles

SIZE

One size fits all (women's)

GAUGE (TENSION)

4 sts x 20 rows to a 4in (10cm) square over stockinette (stocking) stitch, using US size 8 (5mm) needles and Plump Superchunky.

ABBREVIATIONS

approx	approximately
beg	beginning
inc	increase
k	knit
p	purl
PM	place marker
rep	repeat
RS	right side
st(s)	stitch(es)a
WS	wrong side

bright fingerless gloves

If you're going to wear fingerless gloves to keep you warm during winter months, why not go all the way and make them using a superbulky supersoft wool. This wool has superfine merino and alpaca and also comes in some really yummy colors. I have used comparatively small needles for these gloves as I wanted the fit to be quite tight.

Glove

(make 2 the same)

Cuff:

Using MC, cast on 32 sts, PM and join into a round.

Rounds 1–9: K2, p2.

Main part of glove:

Round 10: K to end.

Rep this round until work measures approx 1½in (4cm) from end of ribbing.

Thumb shaping:

Round 1: K2, inc in next st, PM and remove original st marker, k to last 3 sts of new round, PM, inc in next st, k2.

Round 2: K to end.

Round 3: Inc in first st, k to one st before next st marker, inc in next st, slip st marker, k to end.

Round 4: K to end.

Rep Rounds 3 and 4 until there are 40 sts, but on last rep of Round 4, knit to last 5 sts before second st marker, bind (cast) off 12 sts, k to beg of bound (cast)-off stitches, PM, miss bound (cast)-off sts.

Work next 4 rounds in K2, P2 rib.

Bind (cast) off loosely in rib.

Finishing

Use yarn end to neaten edge and sew up slight gap at thumb join.

Using A, make 2 small pompoms (see page 108) and sew onto back of each Glove.

Tip Make stitch markers to denote the thumb gusset in different colors to the stitch marker that marks the beginning of the round, so you recognize the start of each round.

chunky ribbed pompom hat

Who doesn't like a pompom hat! The 2x2 ribbing that's used for this cool version is an excellent stitch when you need stretch, so this one-size hat is suitable for both men and women.

MATERIALS

- Mrs Moon Plump Superchunky, 80% superfine merino, 20% baby alpaca superbulky (superchunky) yarn, 3½oz (100g) skeins, approx 76yd (70m) per skein:
  2 x skeins of Raspberry Ripple (dark pink) (A)
- Debbie Bliss Rialto Chunky, 100% merino wool chunky (bulky) yarn, 1¾oz (50g) balls, approx 66yd (60m) per ball:
  1 x ball of Ecru shade 03 (off white) (B)
- US size 15 (10mm) circular needle, 15¾in (40cm) length
- Yarn sewing needle

SIZE

One size fits all.

FINISHED MEASUREMENTS

Approx 11in (28cm) long (before turn up) x 8½in (21.5cm) high (with turn up)

GAUGE (TENSION)

13 sts x 14 rows to a 4in (10cm) square over 2x2 ribbing, using US size 15 (10mm) needle and Plump Superchunky.

ABBREVIATIONS

beg	beginning
cont	continue
dec	decrease
k	knit
k2tog	knit 2 stitches together
p	purl
PM(s)	place marker(s)
rem	remaining
rep	repeat
st(s)	stitch(es)
WS	wrong side

SPECIAL ABBREVIATION

s2togkpo—with yarn at back, slip 2 stitches together knitwise, knit 1, pass 2 slipped stitches over

Hat

Using A, cast on 48 sts. Work in rounds, PM to denote beg of round.

Round 1: *K2, p2 (ribbing); rep from * to end.

Cont to work in ribbing until Hat measures approx 10in (25.5cm). PMs to divide sts on needle into six equal groups of 8 sts.

Crown shaping:

Round 1: *K2, p1, s2togkpo, p2; rep from * to end of round. (36 sts)

Round 2: *K2, p1, k1, p2; rep from * to end.

Round 3: *K2, s2togkpo, p1; rep from * to end. (24 sts)

Round 4: *K2, p2; rep from * to end.

Round 5: *K1, s2togkpo; rep from * to end. (12 sts)

Round 6: K to end.

Round 7: *K2tog around.

Break yarn leaving a long tail.

Finishing

Thread tail onto yarn sewing needle and thread needle through rem sts and off needle. Pull tight and weave in end on WS of work.

Using B, make a large pompom (see page 108) and sew onto top of Hat.

flower brooch

What a lovely embellishment to a summer cardigan or winter coat! This beaded brooch is the perfect size to make a stylish statement.

MATERIALS

- Debbie Bliss Rialto DK, 100% merino wool light worsted (DK) yarn, 1¾oz (50g) balls, approx 115yd (105m) per ball:
  1 x ball each of:
  Rose shade 76 (pink) (A)
  Citrus shade 69 (yellow) (B)
- US size 3 (3.25mm) knitting needles
- Yarn sewing needle
- Approx 50 pink seed beads size 6
- Sewing needle and matching thread
- Small piece of felt
- 1 brooch pin

SIZE

Approx 4in (10cm) diameter

GAUGE (TENSION)

Exact gauge (tension) is not essential for this project.

ABBREVIATIONS

approx	approximately
k	knit
kfb	knit in front and back of next stitch
k2tog	knit 2 stitches together
LH	left hand
rep	repeat
RH	right hand
st(s)	stitch(es)

Petals

(make 6)
Using A, cast on 8 sts.
Row 1: K2tog, k4, kfb, k. (8 sts)
Row 2: K to end.
Rep first and second rows 3 times, then work first row again.
Bind (cast) off.

Stamens

Using B, cast on 12 sts.
Make a loop on each st as follows: K1 but do not slip st from needle, bring yarn forward between needles, take it clockwise around left thumb and back between needles, knit st on LH needle again, slipping it off in the usual way, on RH needle slip first st over st just made.
Bind (cast) off, working k2tog across row.
Bind (cast) off last st, leaving a long tail.

Finishing

Join Petals together to halfway along inner edges and pinch corner of each end of petal to create a slight tuck. This creates shape of flower. Sew in ends.

Thread tail of Stamen onto yarn sewing needle, join cast-on end to bound (cast)-off end to form a circle of stamen loops and secure end. Sew in ends.

Place Stamen into the center of flower and sew in place.

Sew beads into the center of stamen.

Cut a circular piece of felt. Sew brooch pin into the center of felt piece. Place felt piece onto back of flower using sewing needle and thread.

bracelets

These are great for using up scraps of wool and any spare buttons. A very quick fashion statement, and they also make excellent gifts.

MATERIALS

- Debbie Bliss Baby Cashmerino, 55% wool, 33% acrylic, 12% cashmere sportweight (lightweight DK) yarn, 1¾oz (50g) balls, approx 137yd (125m) per ball:
1 x ball (or scraps) each of:

BRACELET 1
Ecru shade 101 (off white)
Peach Melba shade 68 (peach)
Orange shade 92 (orange)

BRACELET 2
Red shade 34 (red)
Fuchsia shade 88 (pink)
Apple shade 02 (green)

BRACELET 3
Sapphire shade 89 (blue)
Silver shade 12 (gray)
White shade 100 (white)

- US size 4 (3.5mm) double-pointed needles
- Yarn sewing needle
- 1 x button for each bracelet

SIZE

Approx 7in (17.5cm) circumference

GAUGE (TENSION)

Exact gauge (tension) is not essential for this project

ABBREVIATIONS

approx	approximately
k3tog	knit 3 stitches together
rep	repeat
st(s)	stitch(es)

Bracelet cord

(make 1 in each color)
Using two US size 4 (3.5mm) double-pointed needles, cast on 3 sts. *Knit to end. Do not turn. Slide sts to the other end of the needle, keeping the working yarn to the back; rep from * until work measures approx 7in (17.5cm). K3tog, and fasten off.

Finishing

Weave in ends of two of the cords. On the third cord, use the tails to join each end of all three cords together and then join these two ends together to form the bracelet. Sew a button onto the join.

MATERIALS

- Fyberspates Scrumptious 4ply, 55% merino wool, 45% silk fingering (4ply) yarn, 3½oz (100g) skeins, approx 399yd (365m) per skein:
  1 x skein each of:
  Glisten shade 318 (pale gray) (A)
  Gold shade 302 (yellow) (B)
- US size 2/3 (3mm) knitting needles
- Yarn sewing needle
- Bow tie neck strap approx 4in (10cm) diameter

SIZE

4½ x 2½in (11.5 x 6.5cm)
Bow piece approx 9 x 2½in (23 x 6.5cm) before sewing
Center band approx 2½ x 1in (6.5 x 2.5cm) before sewing

GAUGE (TENSION)

Exact gauge (tension) is not essential for this project.

ABBREVIATIONS

approx	approximately
k	knit
p	purl
rep	repeat
RS	right side
st(s)	stitch(es)
WS	wrong side

bow tie

Made in a smooth silk yarn, this is as individual and cool as it gets—it's fit for any gent!

Bow piece

Using A, cast on 18 sts.
Work in seed (moss) st as follows:
Row 1: *K1, p1; rep from * to end.
Row 2: *P1, k1; rep from * to end.
Rep Rows 1 and 2 until 38 rows have been worked. Cut A, join B.
Row 39 (RS): K to end. Cut B, Join A.
Rep Rows 1 and 2 in seed (moss) st until another 31 rows have been worked.
Cut A, join B.
Row 71 (RS): K to end. Cut B, join A.
Rep Rows 1 and 2 in seed (moss) st until another 38 rows have been worked.
Bind (cast) off.

Center band

Using A, cast on 8 sts.
Work in seed (moss) st until work measures 2½in (6.5cm).
Bind (cast) off.

Finishing

Sew in ends.
Fold Bow piece with RS together and join seam.
Turn RS out, and center seam.
Sew running stitch along seam through both layers and pull tight to gather.
Make a running stitch back along the seam, through the gathers to secure.
Wrap Center band and middle of Bow and sew into place at the back.
Loop bow tie strap through center loop at back, and fasten in place.

MATERIALS

- Debbie Bliss Angel, 76% mohair, 24% silk laceweight (2ply) yarn, ⅞oz (25g) balls, approx 218yd (200m) per ball:
  1 x ball each of:
  Acid shade 46 (yellow) (A)
  Charcoal shade 03 (gray) (B)
  Ecru shade 06 (off white) (C)
  Kingfisher shade 23 (blue) (D)
  Basil shade 28 (green) (E)
- US size 6 (4mm) circular needle, 24in (60cm) length

SIZE

13in (33cm) deep x 56in (140cm) around

GAUGE (TENSION)

Approx 22 sts x 28 rows to a 4in (10cm) square over stockinette (stocking) stitch, using US size 6 (4mm) needles and Angel.

ABBREVIATIONS

alt	alternating
approx	approximately
cont	continue
k	knit
p	purl
rep	repeat
RS	right side
st(s)	stitch(es)
st st	stockinette (stocking) stitch
WS	wrong side

striped mohair cowl

I used to not be a fan of mohair because it was too itchy, but this beautiful yarn is soft and silky. This cowl is deliciously thick and is wrapped twice around the neck to make a cozy neck warmer.

Method

Using A, cast on 288 sts, join the round, place marker to denote beginning of round.

Work in st st throughout (every round knit from RS).

Rounds 1–10: K.

Fasten off A, join in B.

K next 10 rounds in B.

Fasten off B, join in C.

K next 10 rounds in C.

Join in D without cutting C.

*Knit one round in D.

Next 8 rounds: Knit, alt C and D on every other st by using opposite color to st in round below.

Knit one round in D*.

Fasten off C and D, join in E.

K next 10 rounds in E.

Fasten off E and join in C and D.

Next 10 rounds: Rep from * to *.

Fasten off D and cont with C.

K next 10 rounds in C.

Fasten off C, change to B.

K next 10 rounds in B.

Fasten off B, change to A.

K last 10 rounds in A.

Bind (cast) off.

Finishing

Weave in ends.

Block and lightly press edges with a damp cloth.

chevron scarf

With so many dark coats around in the winter, this is a really bright and cheerful scarf to make you smile and keep you warm. It also has a lovely textured chevron pattern for extra interest.

MATERIALS

- Mrs Moon Plump DK, 80% superfine merino, 20% baby alpaca worsted yarn, 1¾oz (50g) skeins, approx 126yd (115m) per skein:
  5 x skeins of Lemon Curd
- US size 6 (4mm) knitting needles

SIZE

8in (20cm) wide x 72in (183cm) long

GAUGE (TENSION)

Approx 22 sts x 36 rows to a 4in (10cm) square over pattern, using US size 6 (4mm) needles and Plump DK.

ABBREVIATIONS

approx	approximately
k	knit
p	purl
rep	repeat
RS	right side
st(s)	stitch(es)
WS	wrong side
[ ]	repeat stitches in brackets number of times stated

Scarf

Cast on 45 sts.

Row 1 (RS): K1, *p3, [k1, p1] twice, k1, p5, k1, [p1, k1] twice, p3, k1; rep from * once more.

Row 2: P2, *k3, [p1, k1] twice, p1, k3, p1, [k1, p1] twice, k3, p3; rep from * once more, ending with p2.

Row 3: K3, *p3, [k1, p1] 5 times, k1, p3, k5; rep from * once more, ending with k3.

Row 4: K1, *p3, k3, [p1, k1] 4 times, p1, k3, p3, k1; rep from * once more.

Row 5: P2, *k3, p3, [k1, p1] 3 times, k1, p3, k3, p3; rep from * once more, ending with p2.

Row 6: K3, *p3, k3, [p1, k1] twice, p1, k3, p3, k5; rep from * once more, ending with k3.

Row 7: K1, *p3, k3, p3, k1, p1, k1, p3, k3, p3, k1; rep from * to end.

Row 8: K1, *[p1, k3, p3, k3] twice, p1, k1; rep from * to end.

Row 9: K1, *p1, k1, p3, k3, p5, k3, p3, k1, p1, k1; rep from * to end.

Row 10: K1, *p1, k1, p1, [k3, p3] twice, k3, [p1, k1] twice; rep from * to end.

Row 11: K1, [p1, k1] twice, p3, k3, p1, k3, p3, *[k1, p1] 4 times, k1, p3, k3, p1, k3, p3; rep from * to last 5 sts, [k1, p1] twice, k1.

Row 12: K1, [p1, k1] twice, p1, k3, p5, k3, *[p1, k1] 5 times, p1, k3, p5, k3; rep from * to last 6 sts, [p1, k1] 3 times.

Row 13: P2, *[k1, p1] twice, k1, p3, k3, p3, [k1, p1] twice, k1, p3; rep from * once more, ending with p2.

Row 14: K3, *[p1, k1] twice, [p1, k3] twice, [p1, k1] twice, p1, k5; rep from * once more, ending with k3.

Rep these 14 rows until work measures approx 72in (183cm), ending on a Row 14.

Bind (cast) off.

Finishing

Weave in ends.

mittens

These gorgeous mittens are made with supersoft wool, and are knitted with two strands held together to make the mittens thicker. You can also knit these in Aran weight yarn, using a single strand.

MATERIALS

- Chester Wool Merino Silk DK, 50% superwash merino, 50% silk light worsted (DK) yarn, 3½oz (100g) skeins, approx 109yd (212m) per skein:
  1 x skein of off white (A)
- Chester Wool Angel DK, 70% baby alpaca, 20% silk, 10% cashmere light worsted (DK) yarn, 3½oz (100g) skeins, approx 109yd (225m) per skein:
  1 x skein of light grey (B)
- US size 6 (4mm) and US size 8 (5mm) double-pointed needles
- Yarn sewing needle
- Stitch holder
- Stitch marker to indicate beginning of round
- 2 contrast color stitch markers to indicate space for thumb gusset

SIZE

To fit an average size woman's hand

FINISHED MEASUREMENT

Approx 10in (25cm) long x 4in (10cm) wide

GAUGE (TENSION)

Approx 17 sts x 24 rows to a 4in (10cm) square over stockinette (stocking) stitch, using US size 8 (5mm) needles and two strands held together of Merino Silk DK.

NOTE

Divide each skein of wool into two equal balls—the mittens are worked using yarn doubled throughout. Each mitten is worked in the round using double-pointed needles.

ABBREVIATIONS

approx	approximately
beg	beginning
cont	continue
inc	increase
k	knit
k2tog	knit 2 stitches together
k3tog	knit 3 stitches together
p	purl
PM	place marker
p2tog	purl 2 stitches together
rem	remaining
rep	repeat
RS	right side
SM	slip marker
st(s)	stitch(es)
st st	stockinette (stocking) stitch
WS	wrong side

Mitten

(make 2)

Cuff

Using A and US size 6 (4mm) double-pointed needles, cast on 36 sts. Divide onto 3 needles and join into a ring, taking care not to twist sts. Place marker to indicate beg of round.

Work K1, p1 rib for 17 rounds, or until work measures approx 3in (7.5cm).

Change to US size 8 (5mm) double-pointed needles and work in st st (every round k from RS) for 6 rounds until work measures approx 4in (10cm) from beg.

Thumb shaping

Round 1: Cont with A and US size 8 (5mm) double-pointed needles, k17, inc 1 in next st, k to end. (37 sts)

Round 2: K17, PM (first contrast marker). K3, PM (second contrast marker), k to end.

Round 3: K to first contrast marker, SM, inc 1 in each of next 2 sts, k1 to second contrast marker, SM, k to end. (5 sts between contrast markers)

Round 4: K to end. (5 sts between contrast markers)

Round 5: K to first contrast marker, SM, inc 1 in next st, k to last 2 sts before second contrast marker, inc 1 in next st, k1, SM, k to end. (7 sts between contrast markers)

Round 6: K to end. (7 sts between contrast markers)

Rep Rounds 5 and 6 three times more. (13 sts between contrast markers)

Rep Round 5 once more. (15 sts between contrast markers)

Next round: K to first contrast marker, remove contrast marker, k1, slip next 13 sts onto st holder, k1, remove second contrast marker, k to end.

Work in st st on rem 36 sts until piece measures approx 7½in (19cm) from beg.

Change to B. Work in st st (every round k from RS) for another 8 rounds or approx 1in (2.5cm).

Shape top

Cont using B and US size 8 (5mm) double-pointed needles.

Round 1: *K4, k2tog; rep from * to end. (30 sts)

Round 2: K to end.

Round 3: *K3, k2tog; rep from * to end. (24 sts)

Round 4: K to end.

Round 5: *K2, k2tog; rep from * to end. (18 sts)

Round 6: K to end.

Round 7: *K1, k2tog; rep from * to end. (12 sts)

Round 8: K to end.

Round 9: K2tog around. (6 sts)

Cut yarn, leaving a long tail. Draw tail through rem stitches using yarn sewing needle. Pull tightly and fasten off.

Thumb

Using US size 8 (5mm) double-pointed needles, divide sts from st holder evenly onto 3 needles. Working on RS, join yarn and pick up and k 3 sts along inside edge of hand, k rem stitches. (16 sts) PM to indicate beg of round.

Next round: K3tog, k to end of round. (14 sts)

Work in st st (every round k from RS) for 5 rounds or until Thumb measures approx 2½in (6.5cm).

Next round: *K2tog to end. (7 sts)

Cut yarn, leaving a long tail. Draw tail through rem stitches with yarn sewing needle and pull tightly together to secure. Fasten off.

Finishing

Weave in ends on WS.

headband

If it□s not cold enough for a hat but you need a bit of warmth and style—and you'd like a quick project—then this is perfect for you. Knitted in a superbulky yarn, you'll love making this stylish headband.

MATERIALS

- Debbie Bliss Lara, 58% wool, 42% alpaca superbulky (superchunky) yarn, 3½oz (100g) balls, approx 65yd (60m) per ball:
  1 x ball of Misha shade 05 (beige) (MC)
- Debbie Bliss Rialto DK, 100% merino wool light worsted (DK) yarn, 1¾oz (50g) balls, approx 115yd (105m) per ball:
  1 x ball each of:
  Rose shade 76 (pink) (A)
  Citrus shade 69 (yellow) (B)
- US size 11 (8mm) and US size 6 (4mm) knitting needles
- Pair of US size 8–15 (5–10mm) double-pointed needles (to use as stitch holders)
- Yarn sewing needle

SIZE

Approx 3 x 19in (7.5 x 47.5cm)

GAUGE (TENSION)

14 sts x 13 rows to a 4in (10cm) square over 2x2 rib, using US size 11 (8mm) needles and Lara.

ABBREVIATIONS

approx	approximately
cont	continue
k	knit
kfb	knit in front and back of next stitch
LH	left hand
p	purl
rem	remaining
rep	repeat
RH	right hand
RS	right side
st(s)	stitch(es)
tog	together
WS	wrong side
[ ]	repeat stitches in brackets number of times stated

SPECIAL ABBREVIATIONS

ssk—slip slip knit decrease: slip each of next two sts from left needle to right needle knitwise, insert left needle knitwise in both sts and knit them together

s2togkpo—with yarn at back, slip 2 sts together knitwise, knit 1, pass 2 slipped sts over

Headband

Using US size 11 (8mm) needles and MC, cast on 14 sts.

Row 1: [K2, p2] (rib) to end.

Row 2: [P2, k2] (rib) to end.

Rep Rows 1 and 2 for 26 rows, or approx 7in (17.5cm), ending on Row 2.

Next row: K2, p2, k2, place these 6 sts on a double-pointed needle. Do not cut yarn, but cont on rem sts, and bind (cast) off 2 sts in rib (center), using double-pointed needle as RH needle. After binding (casting) off 2 sts, slip 1 st from RH needle to LH needle (6 sts). K2, p2, k2 using US size 11 (8mm) needle.

Cont in rib on these 6 sts for 16 rows, until work measures approx 4in (10cm) from center. Place these 6 sts on a double-pointed needle. Cut yarn leaving a long tail.

Pick up 6 sts left on first double-pointed needle onto US size 11 (8mm) needle and cont in rib to match other side (starting from center).

With RS facing, cross left group of 6 sts (on double-pointed needle) across other 6 sts, slipping first st from double-pointed needle onto last st on

US size 11 (8mm) needle (this keeps it in place as you turn). Turn.

Starting on WS, work first set of 6 sts in rib, cast on 2 sts (knitting first st from double-pointed needle).

Starting with K2, rib to end. (14 sts) Cont to work in rib on these 14 sts and US size 11 (8mm) needles to match other side. (26 rows, or approx 7in/17.5cm) Bind (cast) off.

Flower

Petals (make 4)
Work in garter st (every row knit).
Using US size 6 (4mm) needles and B, cast on 7 sts.
Row 1 (RS): K.
Row 2: Kfb, k to last 2 sts, kfb, k1. (9 sts)
Row 3: Rep Row 2. (11 sts)
Row 4: Rep Row 2. (13 sts)
Rows 5–8: K.
Row 9: Ssk twice, k to last 4 sts, k2tog twice. (9 sts)
Rows 10–12: K.
Row 13: Rep Row 9. (5 sts)
Rows 14–16: K.
Row 17: K1, s2togkpo, k1. (3 sts)
Row 18: K.
Bind (cast) off.

Center
Using US size 6 (4mm) needles and C, cast on 16 sts.
Bind (cast) off.

Finishing

Weave in ends on WS.

With RS of Headband tog, taking care that crossed pieces in center are twisted neatly, sew cast-on edge to bound (cast) off edge. Turn RS out.

Using A, make a pompom approx 2½in (6.5cm) diameter (see page 108) and sew on RS of Headband at back, slightly off-center (approx 2in/5cm from seam).

Join bound (cast)-off edges of Flower petals tog by first joining two petals tog, followed by joining other two. Place one set on top of other set in cross formation, and sew tog.

Twist Flower center into a spiral and coil. Place into center of Flower petals and sew in place.

Overlap Flower petals and sew them to secure.

Sew Flower approx 2in (5cm) from seam on RS.

chapter four

KNITTED HOME

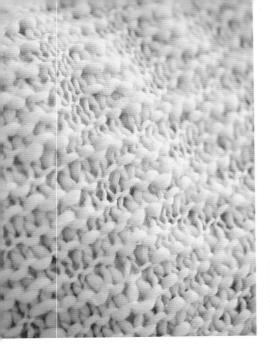

chunky pillow

This yarn is very stretchy, so I made the cover to be slightly smaller than the pillow form so it stretches over it to show off the stitches. This also makes for a nice, plump pillow.

MATERIALS

- Chester Wool Chunky BFL Flame, 96% Blue-faced Leicester, 4% cotton bulky (chunky) yarn, 3½oz (100g) skeins, approx 109yd (100m) per skein:
  4 x skeins of Natural
- US size 15 (10mm) knitting needles
- Yarn sewing needle
- 22in (55cm) pillow form
- Sewing needle and matching thread

SIZE

Approx 18in (45cm) square

GAUGE (TENSION)

Approx 16 rows x 10 sts to a 4in (10cm) square over garter stitch, using US size 15 (10mm) needles and Chunky BFL, before stretching onto pillow form.

NOTE

It is important to work a gauge (tension) square on this as the yarn thickness is variable.

ABBREVIATIONS

approx	approximately
k	knit
WS	wrong side
st(s)	stitch(es)

Pillow

Cast on 48 sts.
Work in garter st (every row knit) until work measures 36in (90cm).
Bind (cast) off.

Finishing

With WS together, fold in half so that cast-on and bound (cast)-off edges meet. Sew side seams, turn RS out, insert pillow form, sew last seam using mattress stitch (see page 107).

MATERIALS

- Debbie Bliss Cotton DK, 100% cotton light worsted (DK) yarn, 1¾oz (50g) balls, approx 92yd (84m) per ball:

MAT 1
1 x ball each of:
Navy Blue shade 18 (dark blue) (A)
Marine shade 76 (turquoise) (B)
Apple shade 69 (light green) (C)

MAT 2
1 x ball each of:
Cloud shade 68 (gray) (A)
Citrus shade 79 (lime green) (B)
Ecru shade 02 (off white) (C)

- US size 8 (5mm) knitting needles
- US size 6 (4mm) double-pointed needles
- Yarn sewing needle

SIZE

Approx 8in (20cm) square

GAUGE (TENSION)

Approx 16 sts x 25 rows to a 4in (10cm) square over garter stitch, using US size 8 (5mm) needles and Cotton DK doubled.

ABBREVIATIONS

approx	approximately
k	knit
k3tog	knit 3 stitches together
st(s)	stitch(es)

pot mats

These are really great mats for protecting your surfaces from hot pots and pans. They're made in a lovely thick cotton yarn, which is knitted with two strands to make them extra chunky.

Mat
Use yarn doubled throughout.
Using US size 8 (5mm) needles and A, cast on 32 sts.
K 16 rows, or until work measures approx 2½in (6.5cm).
Cut A, join B, k 16 rows, or for approx 2½in (6.5cm).
Cut B, join C, k 16 rows, or for approx 2½in (6.5cm).
Bind (cast) off.

Tab
Using a single strand of yarn and two US size 6 (4mm) double-pointed needles, cast on 3 sts. *Knit to end. Do not turn. Slide stitches to the other end of the needle, keeping the working yarn to the back; rep from * until cord measures approx 5in (12.5cm).
K3tog, and fasten off.

Finishing
Fold Tab in half to make a loop and sew onto one corner of Mat.
Weave in ends.

book cover

When I was a child, we would cover our schoolbooks with old wallpaper to protect them and make them more individual. Here is the same idea, but knitted in a lovely textured stitch.

MATERIALS

COVER
- Debbie Bliss Rialto DK, 100% merino wool light worsted (DK) yarn, 1¾oz (50g) balls, approx 115yd (105m) per ball:
  1 x ball of Jade shade 71 (green)

POMPOMS
- Debbie Bliss Falkland Aran, 100% wool worsted (Aran) yarn, 3½oz (100g) balls, approx 197yd (180m) per ball:
  1 x ball of Mustard shade 07 (yellow)

- US size 6 (4mm) knitting needles
- Yarn sewing needle

SIZE

The pattern measurements are for a 8½ x 6in (21.5 x 15cm) book

GAUGE (TENSION)

22 sts x 32 rows to a 4in (10cm) square over double seed (moss) stitch, using US size 6 (4mm) needles and Rialto DK.

NOTE

If your gauge (tension) is different or you need to make a larger or smaller cover, the double seed (moss) stitch multiples are 2 sts + 1 st.

ABBREVIATIONS

approx	approximately
k	knit
p	purl
rep	repeat
RS	right side
st(s)	stitch(es)
WS	wrong side

Method
Cast on 49 sts.
Work in double seed (moss) st as follows:
Row 1: K1, *p1, k1; rep from * to end.
Row 2: P1, *k1, p1; rep from * to end.
Row 3: Rep Row 2.
Row 4: Rep Row 1.
Rep rows 1–4 until work measures 16in (40cm).
Bind (cast) off.

Finishing
With WS facing, fold each short end in by 2in (5cm) and sew edges together to form the two inside pockets.

Turn RS out. Insert cover of book cover into pockets.

Bookmark
Make 2 small pompoms (see page 109). Using three strands of yarn, make a braid (plait) the length of the spine. Attach one pompom at each end.

Tip If you find that the knitting is sliding around on the cover of the book, place a thin layer of glue or double-stick tape along the edges to keep it in place.

Tip If you find picking up stitches is stiff with a knitting needle, try picking up each stitch with a crochet hook and slipping it onto the knitting needle.

egg baskets

Baskets for keeping all your eggs in—and also anything else that needs a pretty container.

MATERIALS

- DMC Natura XL, 100% cotton superbulky (superchunky) yarn, 3½oz (100g) balls, approx 82yd (75m) per ball:
  1 x ball (small size) or 2 x balls (large size) of:
  01 (white) OR 81 (dark teal) OR 83 (yellow)
- US size 6 (4mm) and US size 10 (6mm) knitting needles
- Yarn sewing needle

SIZE

Small: approx 5 x 3in (12.5 x 7.5cm)
Large: approx 5 x 4in (12.5 x 10cm)

GAUGE (TENSION)

11 sts x 16 rows to a 4in (10cm) square over stockinette (stocking) stitch, using US size 10 (6mm) needles and Natura XL doubled.

ABBREVIATIONS

approx	approximately
k	knit
p	purl
rep	repeat
RS	right side
st(s)	stitch(es)
st st	stockinette (stocking) stitch

Base

Use yarn doubled throughout.
Using US size 10 (6mm) needles and any color, cast on 15 sts.
Work in st st for 15 rows.
Bind (cast) off.

Sides

With RS of st st facing, pick up 15 sts on one side.
Starting with a knit row, work 10 rows in st st.
Work 5 rows more in st st for a deeper basket.
Bind (cast) off using US size 6 (4mm) needles.
Rep for other 3 sides.

Finishing

With RS facing, join each corner seam using one strand of yarn and a yarn sewing needle.

bobble pillow cover

I love this stitch, as it's really thick and cozy and perfect for a throw pillow. Adding some bright buttons sets the the blue of the pillow off, too.

MATERIALS

- Debbie Bliss Falkland Aran, 100% wool worsted (Aran) yarn, 3½oz (100g) balls, approx 197yd (180m) per ball:
  6 x balls of Teal shade 10 (blue)
- US size 8 (5mm) knitting needles
- Yarn sewing needle
- 3 buttons
- 16in (40cm) pillow form

SIZE

16 x 16in (40 x 40cm)

GAUGE (TENSION)

Approx 4½ bobbles x 24 bobble rows to a 4in (10cm) square, using US size 8 (5mm) needles and Falkland Aran.

ABBREVIATIONS

approx	approximately
cont	continue
k	knit
p	purl
patt	pattern
rep	repeat
RS	right side
st(s)	stitch(es)
WS	wrong side
yo	yarn over needle
yrn	yarn round needle

SPECIAL ABBREVIATION

bobble—make a bobble: start to knit next st, but do not slide st off needle, yo (to front), insert needle in st again knitwise, yrn and knit st, but do not slide st off needle, yo (to front), insert needle in st again knitwise, yrn and knit st, slide st off needle to finish st (5 sts). Turn work, yo (to back), knit these 5 stitches. Turn work, yo (to back), knit next two sts tog, slip this knitted st rom RH needle onto LH needle, slip each of next three sts over knitted st separately, knit this st to complete bobble

Tip *You may need an 18in (45cm) pillow form as there is "stretch" in this pattern stitch, so best to buy the pillow form once you have made the cover.*

Pillow back

Cast on 77 sts.

Row 1: K to end.

Row 2: P to end.

Row 3: K2, bobble in next st, *k3, bobble in next st: rep from * to last 2 sts, k2.

Row 4: P to end.

Row 5: K4, bobble in next st, *k3, bobble in next st; rep from * to last 4 sts, k4.

Row 6: P to end.

Rep Rows 3–6 until work measures approx 16in (40cm).

Next row: P to end.

Bind (cast) off.

Front top

Cast on 77 sts.

Row 1: K to end.

Row 2: P to end.

Row 3: K2, bobble in next st, *k3, bobble in next st: rep from * to last 2 sts, k2.

Row 4: P to end.

Row 5: K4, bobble in next st, *k3, bobble in next st; rep from * to last 4 sts, k4.

Row 6: P to end.

Rep Rows 3–6 until work measures approx 6in (15cm).

Next row: P to end.

Seed (moss) stitch buttonhole band:

Row 1: K1, *p1, k1; rep to end.

Rep Row 1 (seed/moss st) 3 times.

Row 5: Seed (moss) st 18 sts, bind (cast) off 3 sts, seed (moss) st 16 sts, bind (cast) off 3 sts, seed (moss) st 16 sts, bind (cast) off 3 sts, seed (moss) st 17 sts (one st already worked in bind/cast off).

(3 buttonholes worked)

Row 6: Work in seed (moss) st as set, casting on 3 sts across each buttonhole and working sts as they appear. (77 sts)

Rows 7–8: Seed (moss) st to end.

Bind (cast) off.

Front bottom

Cast on 77 sts.

Work in seed (moss) st for 8 rows (approx 1in/2.5cm).

Beg bobble st patt.

Row 1: K to end.

Row 2: P to end.

Row 3: K2, bobble in next st, *k3, bobble in next st: rep from * to last 2 sts, K2.

Row 4: P to end.

Row 5: K4, bobble in next st, *k3, bobble in next st; rep from * to last 4 sts, k4.

Row 6: P to end.

Rep Rows 3–6 until bobble section measures approx 9in (23cm), plus 1in (2.5cm) of seed (moss) stitch, so approx 10in (25cm) in total.

Next row: P to end.

Bind (cast) off.

Finishing

Place Front bottom onto Pillow back with RS together, aligning side and bottom edges and with seed (moss) st border at the top. Sew together along sides and bottom edge, leaving seed (moss) stitch border unsewn. Place Front top RS down with edges aligned and with seed (moss) st buttonhole band overlapping Front bottom. Sew together along sides and top edge, leaving seed (moss) stitch buttonhole band unsewn.

Turn cover RS out.

Arrange Front top seed (moss) stitch buttonhole band to overlap Front bottom seed (moss) stitch border, and sew together on each side.

Sew buttons in place on Front bottom seed (moss) st border to match buttonholes.

place mats

I'm one of those "throw the plates and cutlery in the middle of the table and help yourself" kinds of people. But every now and then I like to lay a more fancy table, and these homemade place mats go perfectly with my rustic style.

MATERIALS

- DMC Natura XL, 100% cotton superbulky (superchunky) yarn, 3½oz (100g) balls, approx 82yds (75m) per ball:
  6 x balls of shade 32 (stone) (MC)
  1 x ball each of:
  43 (deep pink) (A)
  09 (bright yellow) (B)
  10 (orange) (C)
  81 (dark teal) (D)
  07 (light green) (E)
  42 (peach) (F)
- US size 8 (5mm) knitting needles

SIZE

Approx 12 x 8in (30 x 20.5cm)

GAUGE (TENSION)

15 sts x 30 rows over a 4in (10cm) square over garter stitch, using US size 8 (5mm) needles and Natura XL

ABBREVIATIONS

approx	approximately
k	knit
st(s)	stitch(es)
WS	wrong side

NOTES

Each mat is knitted in garter st (every row knit) mainly in the main color, with an approx 2in (5cm) wide stripe in a contrast color.
Always join a new color on the right side.
To make neat edges, slip the first stitch and knit into the back of the stitch on the last stitch of the row, except when joining the first stitch in a new color.

Mat 1

Using MC, cast on 46 sts.

K 6 rows.

Fasten off MC, join A.

Knit 14 rows.

Fasten off A, join MC.

K 41 rows.

Bind (cast) off on WS.

Mat 2

Using B, cast on 46 sts.

K 12 rows.

Fasten off B, join MC.

K 49 rows.

Bind (cast) off on WS.

Mat 3

Using MC, cast on 46 sts.

K 48 rows.

Fasten off MC, join C.

K 13 rows.

Bind (cast) off on WS.

Mat 4

Using MC, cast on 46 sts.

K 24 rows.

Fasten off MC, join D.

Knit 14 rows.

Fasten off D, join MC.

K 23 rows.

Bind (cast) off on WS.

Mat 5

Using MC, cast on 46 sts.

K 34 rows.

Fasten off MC, join E.

Knit 14 rows.

Fasten off E, join MC.

K 13 rows.

Bind (cast) off on WS.

Mat 6

Using MC, cast on 46 sts.

K 12 rows.

Fasten off MC, join F.

Knit 14 rows.

Fasten off F, join MC.

K 35 rows.

Bind (cast) off on WS.

Finishing

Weave in any ends. Block and press lightly with a damp cloth on WS.

egg cozies

Keep your boiled eggs warm with these little knitted hats—they are very cute, and great to give as gifts. Alternatively, they also make brilliant bottle top covers.

MATERIALS

- Debbie Bliss Rialto 4ply, 100% merino wool fingering (4ply) yarn 1¾oz (50g) balls, approx 197yd (180m) per ball:
  1 x ball (or small amount) each of:
  Amber shade 39 (yellow)
  Pale Blue shade 12 (pale blue)
  Rose shade 44 (bright pink)
  Leaf shade 49 (green)
  Coral shade 55 (orange)
  Mallow shade 43 (purple)
- US size 2/3 (3mm) knitting needles
- Yarn sewing needle

SIZE

To fit an average size egg

GAUGE (TENSION)

Exact gauge (tension) is not essential for this project.

ABBREVIATIONS

approx	approximately
k	knit
RS	right side
st(s)	stitch(es)
WS	wrong side

Cozy

(make 1 in each color)
Cast on 16 sts, knit in garter st (every row knit) for 52 rows, ending on a WS row.
Bind (cast) off.

Finishing

With RS together, sew side seams. Turn RS out.

Make two small fork pompoms (see page 109) for each cozy in a contrasting color. Sew a pompom to the top corner of each cozy.

cafetière cover

I think it's important to have a cafetière cover in a thick stitch to help keep your coffee warm. So in this pattern I've used a worsted (Aran) yarn, which is knitted doubled throughout. The little shell rib stitch also makes a lovely thick fabric—I love this stitch because it looks like a little cable, without having to use a cable needle.

MATERIALS

- Debbie Bliss Cashmerino Aran, 55% merino wool, 33% acrylic, 12% cashmere worsted (Aran) yarn, 1¾oz (50g) balls, approx 98yd (90m) per ball:
  2 x balls of Hot Pink shade 68 (bright pink)
- US size 10 (6mm) knitting needles
- US size 6 (4mm) double-pointed needles
- Yarn sewing needle
- 1 button, ⅞in (20mm) diameter
- 2 buttons, ⅝in (15mm) diameter
- Sewing needle and matching thread

SIZE

Approx 12in (31cm) around x 7in (17.5cm) high
To fit a medium-size 4–6 cup cafetière, approx 12in (31cm) circumference

GAUGE (TENSION)

4 pattern reps x 15 rows to a 4in (10cm) square over little shell rib stitch, using US size 10 (6mm) needles and Cashmerino Aran doubled.

ABBREVIATIONS

approx	approximately
k	knit
k2tog	knit 2 stitches together
p	purl
psso	pass slipped stitch over
rep	repeat
RS	right side
sl	slip
st(s)	stitch(es)
st st	stocking (stockinette) stitch
WS	wrong side
yb	yarn back
[ ]	repeat stitches in brackets number of times stated

Cover

Using US size 10 (6mm) needles and yarn doubled, cast on 62 sts.
Row 1 (RS): P2, *k3, p2; rep from * to end.
Row 2: K2, *p3, k2; rep from * to end.
Row 3: P2, *yb, sl 1, k2tog, psso, p2; rep from * to end.
Row 4: K2, *[p1, k1, p1] all in same st, k2; rep from * to end.
Rep Rows 1–4 for 7in (17.5cm), ending on a Row 3.
Bind (cast) off.

Top tab

With RS facing, using US size 6 (4mm) double-pointed needle and one strand of yarn only, join yarn at bound (cast)-off edge (top of Cover). Pick up in another loop at bound (cast)-off edge. (2 sts)
*Knit to end. Do not turn. Slide sts to other end of needle, keeping working yarn to back; rep from * until work measures approx 3½in (9cm).
Bind (cast) off.

Using yarn sewing needle and thread, join end in same st as cast on.

Cut yarn and sew in ends.

With RS together, and one strand of yarn, sew approx 1in (2.5cm) of bottom seam of cover.

Middle tab

Measure approx 2½in (6.5cm) from top down side edge and, *using US size 6 (4mm) double-pointed needle, with RS facing, join yarn in edge. Slide loop to other end of needle. (1 st)

**Knit to end. Do not turn. Slide sts to other end of needle, keeping working yarn to back; rep from ** until work measures approx 2in (5cm). (approx 10 sts), fasten off.

Bind (cast) off.

Using yarn sewing needle and thread, join end in next st along from cast on.

Cut yarn and sew in ends.

Bottom tab

Measure approx 1in (2.5cm) from where seam ends; rep Middle tab from *.

Finishing

Sew ⅞in (20mm) button on top edge to match Top tab, sew ⅝in (15mm) buttons on opposite edge to match Middle tab and Bottom tab.

 Turn RS out.

MATERIALS

POUCHES
- Debbie Bliss Baby Cashmerino, 55% wool, 33% acrylic, 12% cashmere sportweight (lightweight DK) yarn, 1¾oz (50g) balls, approx 137yd (125m) per ball:
1 x ball of Butter shade 83 (yellow) OR Pool shade 71 (blue) OR Baby Pink shade 601 (pale pink) OR Rose Pink shade 94 (pink) (MC)

BOWS
1 x ball of Lilac shade 10 (A)
- US size 2/3 (3mm) knitting needles
- Yarn sewing needle
- Dried aromatic lavender

SIZE

Approx 3 x 3½in (7.5 x 9cm)

GAUGE (TENSION)

Exact gauge (tension) is not essential for this project.

ABBREVIATIONS

approx	approximately
k	knit
p	purl
rep	repeat
RS	right side
st(s)	stitch(es)

lavender pouches

Sometimes the simplest things are the best—and sometimes knitted projects can be made just for the pleasure of making. These lavender pouches are one of those things for me, and they also make lovely gifts.

Pouches

Using MC, cast on 21 sts.
Row 1: *K1, p1: rep from * to end.
Rep Row 1 (seed/moss st) until work measures approx 6½in (16.5cm).
Bind (cast) off.

Bow

(make 1 for each pouch)
Using A, cast on 8 sts.
Knit 16 rows (garter st).
Bind (cast) off, leaving long tail.

Finishing

With RS together, fold Pouch in half and sew side seams (with the fold at bottom).
Turn RS out. Fill with lavender and sew top seam using mattress stitch (see page 107).

With RS of Bow together, sew seam lengthwise. Turn RS out.

Sew in cast-on end. Sew long tail along seam to center, do not cut.

Keeping seam at back in center, use long tail to wrap around center 3 or 4 times to create bow shape. Push needle through to back and secure end, do not cut end. Use tail to sew Bow onto center of Pouch.

knitting basics

In this section you'll find the basic knitting techniques that you will need for most of the patterns in this book.

The knitting needles, yarn, and other items that you need are listed at the beginning of each of the pattern instructions. You can substitute the yarn recommended in a pattern with the same weight of yarn in a different brand, but you will need to check the gauge (tension). When calculating the quantity of yarn you require, it is the length of yarn in each ball that you need to check, rather than the weight of the ball; the length of yarn per ball in each recommended project yarn is given in the pattern.

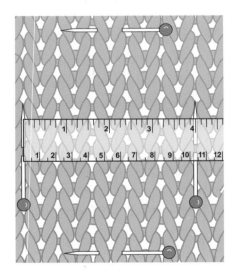

GAUGE (TENSION)

A gauge (tension) is given with each pattern to help you make your item the same size as the sample. The gauge is given as the number of stitches and rows you need to work to produce a 4-in (10-cm) square of knitting.

Using the recommended yarn and needles, cast on 8 stitches more than the gauge (tension) instruction asks for—so if you need to have 10 stitches to 4in (10cm), cast on 18 stitches. Working in pattern as instructed, work eight rows more than is needed. Bind (cast) off loosely.

Lay the swatch flat without stretching it. Lay a ruler across the stitches as shown, with the 2in (5cm) mark centered on the knitting, then put a pin in the knitting at the start of the ruler and at the 4in (10cm) mark:

the pins should be well away from the edges of the swatch. Count the number of stitches between the pins. Repeat the process across the rows to count the number of rows to 4in (10cm).

If the number of stitches and rows you've counted is the same as the number asked for in the instructions, you have the correct gauge (tension). If you do not have the same number then you will need to change your gauge (tension).

To change gauge (tension) you need to change the size of your knitting needles. A good rule of thumb to follow is that one difference in needle size will create a difference of one stitch in the gauge (tension). You will need to use larger needles to achieve fewer stitches and smaller ones to achieve more stitches.

HOLDING NEEDLES

If you are a knitting novice, you will need to discover which is the most comfortable way for you to hold your needles.

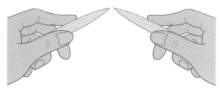

Like a knife

Pick up the needles, one in each hand, as if you were holding a knife and fork—that is to say, with your hands lightly over the top of each needle. As you knit, you will tuck the blunt end of the right-hand needle under your arm, let go with your hand and use your hand to manipulate the yarn, returning your hand to the needle to move the stitches along.

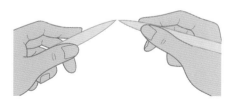

Like a pen

Now try changing the right hand so you are holding the needle as you would hold a pen, with your thumb and forefinger lightly gripping the needle close to its pointed tip and the shaft resting in the crook of your thumb. As you knit, you will not need to let go of the needle but simply slide your right hand forward to manipulate the yarn.

HOLDING YARN

As you knit, you will be working stitches off the left needle and onto the right needle, and the yarn you are working with needs to be tensioned and manipulated to produce an even fabric. To hold and tension the yarn you can use either your right or left hand. Try both methods to discover which works best for you.

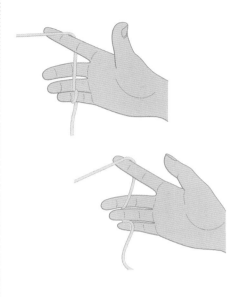

Yarn in right hand

To knit and purl in the US/UK style (see pages 101 and 102), hold the yarn in your right hand.
To hold the yarn tightly (top), wind it right around your little finger, under your ring and middle fingers, then pass it over your index finger; this finger will manipulate the yarn.
For a looser hold (bottom), catch the yarn between your little and ring fingers, pass it under your middle finger, then over your index finger.

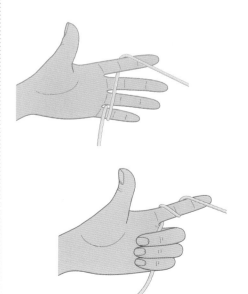

Yarn in left hand

To knit and purl in the continental style (see pages 101 and 102), hold the yarn in your left hand.
To hold the yarn tightly (top), wind it right around your little finger, under your ring and middle fingers, then pass it over your index finger; this finger will manipulate the yarn.
For a looser hold (bottom), fold your little, ring, and middle fingers over the yarn, and wind it twice around your index finger.

MAKING A SLIP KNOT

You will need to make a slip knot to start knitting; this knot counts as the first cast-on stitch.

1 With the ball of yarn to the right, lay the end of the yarn on the palm of your left hand. With your right hand, wind the yarn twice around your index and middle fingers to make a loop. Make a second loop behind the first one. Slip a knitting needle in front of the first loop to pick up the second loop, as shown.

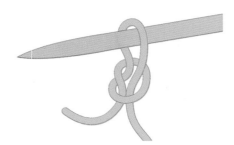

2 Slip the yarn off your fingers, leaving the loop on the needle. Gently pull on both yarn ends to tighten the knot a little, then pull on the yarn leading to the ball of yarn to fully tighten the knot on the needle.

CASTING ON (CABLE METHOD)

There are a few methods of casting on, but the one used for most projects in this book is the cable method, which uses two needles.

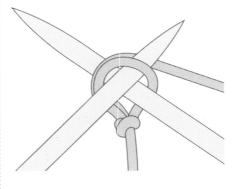

1 Make a slip knot as outlined above. Put the needle with the slip knot into your left hand. Insert the point of your other needle into the front of the slip knot and under the left needle. Wind the yarn from the ball of yarn around the tip of the right needle.

2 Using the tip of your needle, draw the yarn through the slip knot to form a loop. This loop is your new stitch. Slip the loop from the right needle onto the left needle.

3 To make the next stitch, insert the tip of your right needle between the two stitches. Wind the yarn over the right needle, from left to right, then draw the yarn through to form a loop. Transfer this loop to your left needle. Repeat until you have cast on the right number of stitches for your project.

MAKING A KNIT STITCH

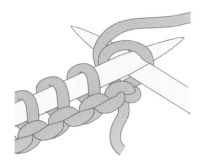

1 Hold the needle with the cast-on stitches in your left hand, and then insert the tip of the right needle into the front of the first stitch, from left to right. Wind the yarn around the point of the right needle, from left to right.

2 With the tip of your right needle, pull the yarn through the stitch to form a loop. This loop is your new stitch.

3 Slip the original stitch off the left needle by gently pulling your right needle to the right. Repeat these steps until you have knitted all the stitches on your left needle. To work the next row, transfer the needle with all the stitches into your left hand.

MAKING A KNIT STITCH—CONTINENTAL STYLE

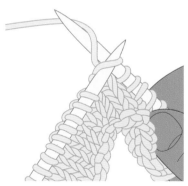

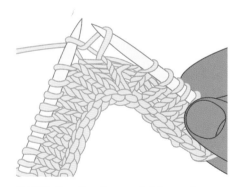

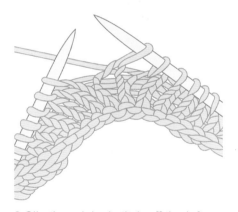

1 Hold the needle with the stitches to be knitted in your left hand, and then insert the tip of the right needle into the front of the first stitch from left to right. Holding the yarn fairly taut with your left hand at the back of your work, use the tip of your right needle to pick up a loop of yarn.

2 With the tip of your right needle, bring the yarn through the original stitch to form a loop. This loop is your new stitch.

3 Slip the original stitch off the left needle by gently pulling your right needle to the right. Repeat these steps until you have knitted all the stitches on your left needle. To work the next row, transfer the needle with all the stitches into your left hand.

MAKING A PURL STITCH

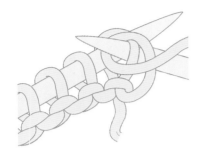  

1 Hold the needle with the stitches in your left hand, and then insert the tip of the right needle into the front of the first stitch, from right to left. Wind the yarn around the point of the right needle, from right to left.

2 With the tip of the right needle, pull the yarn through the stitch to form a loop. This loop is your new stitch.

3 Slip the original stitch off the left needle by gently pulling your right needle to the right. Repeat these steps until you have purled all the stitches on your left needle. To work the next row, transfer the needle with all the stitches into your left hand.

MAKING A PURL STITCH—CONTINENTAL STYLE

 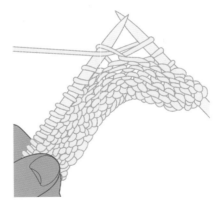 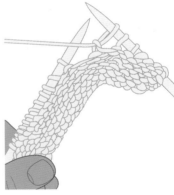

1 Hold the needle with the stitches to be knitted in your left hand, and then insert the tip of the right needle into the front of the first stitch from right to left. Holding the yarn fairly taut at the back of your work, use the tip of your right needle to pick up a loop of yarn.

2 With the tip of your right needle, bring the yarn through the original stitch to form a loop.

3 Slip the original stitch off the left needle by gently pulling your right needle to the right. Repeat these steps until you have purled all the stitches on your left needle. To work the next row, transfer the needle with all the stitches into your left hand.

BINDING (CASTING) OFF

In most cases, you will bind (cast) off knitwise, which means that you will knit the stitches before you bind (cast) them off.

1 First knit two stitches in the normal way. With the point of your left needle, pick up the first stitch you have just knitted and lift it over the second stitch. Knit another stitch so that there are two stitches on your needle again. Repeat the process of lifting the first stitch over the second stitch. Continue this process until there is just one stitch remaining on the right needle.

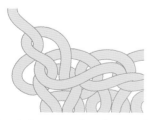

2 Break the yarn, leaving a tail of yarn long enough to stitch your work together. Pull the tail all the way through the last stitch. Slip the stitch off the needle and pull it fairly tightly to make sure it is secure.

STOCKINETTE (STOCKING) STITCH

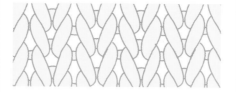

This stitch makes a fabric that is different on each side; the knit side is flat and the purl side is textured. To make this stitch, work alternate rows of knit and purl stitches. The front of the fabric is the side on which to work the knit rows.

GARTER STITCH

This stitch forms a ridged fabric that is the same on both sides. To make this stitch, you simply knit every row.

RIBBING

On an odd number of stitches, alternate knit and purl to the last stitch, and knit the last stitch. On the next row, alternate purl and knit to the last stitch, and purl the last stitch. The smooth and ridged stitches line up to make a reversible elastic fabric.

JOINING IN A NEW COLOR

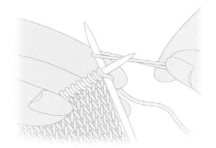

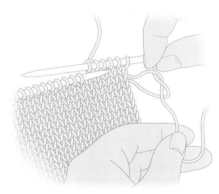

You will usually bring in a new color (as directed in the pattern or chart) at the beginning of the row/round. Break the old yarn, leaving a 4–6in (10–15cm) tail. Insert the needle into the next stitch to be knitted, then knit in the new color as usual, leaving a 4–6in (10–15cm) tail. These tails can be tied together to hold them in position and to stop the loose stitch from falling off the needle. I usually knit one or two stitches before I tie them in place. Never tie in a double knot, because this will make it difficult to sew in the end later and the knot will eventually work itself out of your work.

YARN ROUND NEEDLE (yrn)

This is a way of creating an extra purl stitch between two existing stitches. Bring the yarn from the front to the back of your work, between your two needles. Purl the next stitch (or stitches) in the normal way, taking your yarn over the top of your right-hand needle as you do so to create the additional stitch.

SEED (MOSS) STITCH

To make this stitch, knit and purl alternate stitches across a row. On the next row, knit the knit stitches and purl the purl stitches to create a firm, textured pattern.

INCREASING

A few methods of increasing are used in this book.

Make 1

Pick up the horizontal strand between two stitches on your left-hand needle. Knit into the back of the loop and transfer the stitch to the right-hand needle in the normal way. (It is important to knit into the back of the loop so that the yarn is twisted and does not form a hole in your work.)

Increase 1

Start knitting your stitch in the normal way but instead of slipping the "old" stitch off the needle, knit into the back of it and then slip the "old" stitch off the needle in the normal way.

Knit in front and back of next stitch (kfb)

This creates an extra stitch, so it is also sometimes abbreviated as "inc" in a knitting pattern. There will be a visible bar of yarn across the base of the extra stitch.

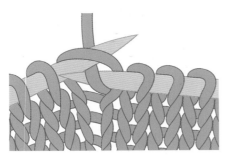

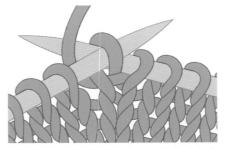

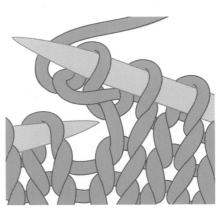

1 Knit the next stitch on the left-hand needle in the usual way, but do not slip the original stitch off the left-hand needle.

2 Move the right-hand needle behind the left-hand needle and put it into the same stitch again, but through the back of the stitch this time. Knit the stitch through the back loop (see right).

3 Slip the original stitch off the left-hand needle. You have increased by one stitch.

Purl in front and back of next stitch (pfb)

This creates an extra stitch, so is also sometimes abbreviated as "inc" when working a purl row, or "inc purlwise."

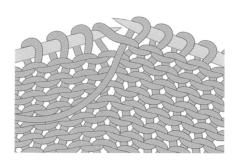

1 Purl the next stitch on the left-hand needle in the usual way, but do not slip the original stitch off the left-hand needle.

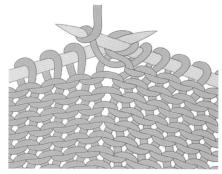

2 Twist the right-hand needle backward to make it easier to put it into the same stitch again, but through the back of the stitch this time. Purl the stitch through the back loop (see below).

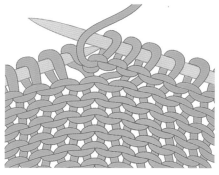

3 Slip the original stitch off the left-hand needle. You have increased by one stitch.

THROUGH THE BACK LOOP

You usually knit or purl stitches by putting the right-hand needle into the front of the stitch. However, sometimes a stitch needs to be twisted to create an effect or to work a technique, and to do this you knit or purl into the back of it. This is called working "through the back loop" and is abbreviated to "tbl" in a knitting pattern.

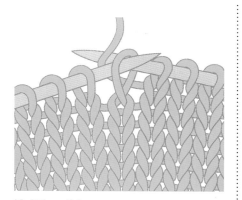

Knitting tbl
Put the right-hand needle into the back of the next stitch on the left-hand needle. Knit the stitch in the usual way, but through the back loop.

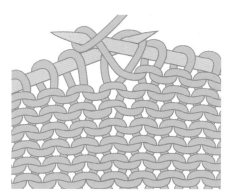

Purling tbl
Put the right-hand needle into the next stitch on the left-hand needle. Purl the stitch in the usual way, but through the back loop.

DECREASING

There are several ways of decreasing.

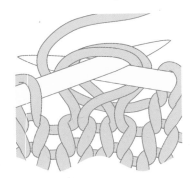

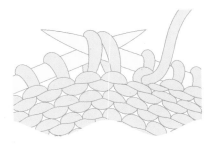

Knit 2 together (k2tog)

This is the simplest way of decreasing. Simply insert your needle through two stitches instead of the normal one when you begin your stitch and then knit them in the normal way.

Purl 2 together (p2tog)

Simply insert your needle through two stitches instead of one when you begin your stitch and then purl them in the normal way.

Purl 2 stitches together through the back loops (p2tog tbl)

Starting at the back of the work, insert the right needle into the back of the next two stitches, from left to right. This will feel counter-intuitive but it is correct; the needle will emerge toward the front. Then purl the two stitches together from this position.

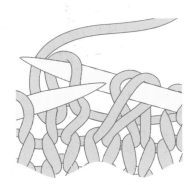

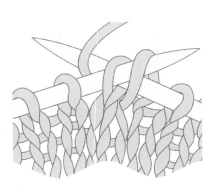

s2togkpo

With yarn at back, slip two stitches together knitwise, knit the next stitch, then pass the two slipped stitches over.

ssk

Slip one stitch and then the next stitch knitwise onto your right-hand needle, without knitting them. Then insert the left-hand needle from left to right through the front loops of both the slipped stitches and knit them together.

KNITTING WITH BEADS

It is easier to work with beads on purl stitches, seed (moss), or garter stitch, because the horizontal bar of the purl stitch lends itself to the addition of a bead. You can purl any stitches that have a bead attached, even if the unbeaded surrounding stitches are all knit stitches, because the bead itself will hide the odd purl stitch.

If your yarn is thin enough to accommodate the holes in your beads, loop the yarn through a small length of sewing cotton and then thread both ends of the cotton into a sewing needle. Push the beads onto the needle and then down onto the yarn in sequence.

If your yarn is too thick for the holes in the beads, then thread the beads onto fine sewing thread and wind this back up into a spool. Knit the beaded thread together with the main yarn.

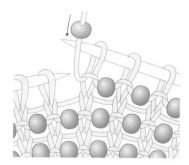

To knit with beads, work as normal up to the first point where a bead is indicated. Work the next stitch, then bring a bead to the front of the work, and work the next stitch to secure it in position, ensuring that the bead sits on the front of the work.

JOINING
Mattress stitch

There are two versions of this stitch—one used to join two vertical edges and the other used to join two horizontal edges.

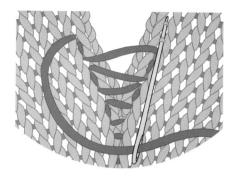

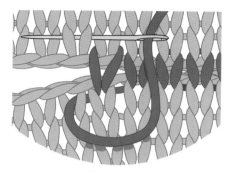

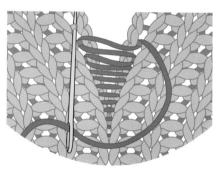

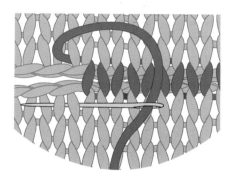

Vertical edges: Place the two edges side by side, with the right side facing you. Take your needle under the running thread between the first two stitches of one side, then under the corresponding running thread of the other side. Pull your yarn up fairly firmly every few stitches.

Horizontal edges: Place the two edges side by side, with the right side facing you. Take your needle under the two "legs" of the last row of stitches on the first piece of knitting. Then take your needle under the two "legs" of the corresponding stitch on the second piece of knitting. Pull your yarn up fairly firmly every few stitches.

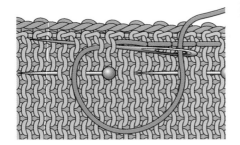

Backstitch seam

This seam is made with right sides facing. Carefully match pattern to pattern, row to row, and stitch to stitch. Sew along the seam using backstitch, sewing into the center of each stitch to correspond with the stitch on the opposite piece. Sew as close in from the edge of the knitting as possible to avoid a bulky seam.

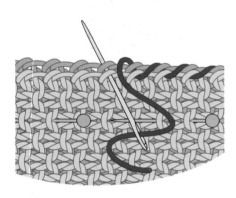

Whipstitch

This stitch is used to seam small pieces of work. It is normally worked with the right sides of your work together. Take the yarn from the back of your work, over the edge of the seam and out through the back again a short distance further on.

BOBBLE STITCH

A bobble is created by increasing several times into the same stitch, then decreasing in the following row.

By increasing just once into a stitch, then decreasing in the following row, you will create a tiny indent of texture. Increasing more than once into the same stitch produces a larger physical area for the bobble. You can widen the increased area to include two or more stitches, and/or work several rows of short rowing over the increased stitches, before decreasing, which will create a defined ridge or bobble.

MAKING POMPOMS

Book method

Use this method to make large pompoms.

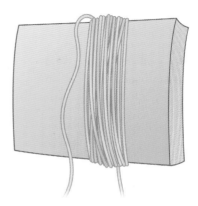

1 Leaving a long tail, wrap the yarn around a paperback book (or something a similar size) about 120 times, leaving a second long tail.

2 Ease the wrapped yarn off the book gently and wrap the second tail tightly around the center six or seven times.

3 Take a yarn sewing needle and thread in the second tail. Push the needle through the center wrap backward and forward three or four times.

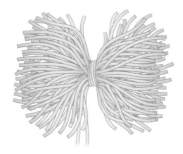

4 Cut the loops on each side of the wrap. Holding the two tails in one hand, hold the bobble and fluff it out.

5 Hold the bobble in one hand and use sharp scissors to trim it into a round and even shape.

Fork method

For smaller pompoms, use this fun method.

1 Keeping the yarn attached to the ball, wrap it around a fork about twenty times. Keep the wraps tight, and center them in the middle of the fork, leaving space at the top and bottom.

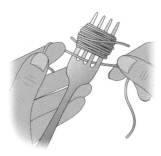

2 Cut the yarn and hold the wraps in place on the fork. Cut a 3in (7.5cm) length of yarn and thread it through the middle of the fork at the bottom from front to back.

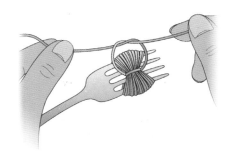

3 Wrap one end around and back over the top until the ends meet, then tie them tightly together at the front. Wrap the tie around the center a few more times and tie another knot at the back.

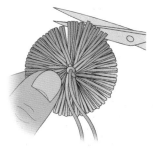

4 Pull the wrap off the fork and pull the knot tighter. The wrap will begin to curl and turn flat and round. Tie another knot on top of the other one to secure. Use sharp embroidery scissors to cut the loops on either side of the tie.

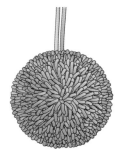

5 Trim the pompom and fluff it up until it's thick and a round, even shape.

EMBROIDERY STITCHES

When embroidering on knitting, take the embroidery needle in and out of the work between the strands that make up the yarn rather than between the knitted stitches themselves; this will help make your embroidery look more even.

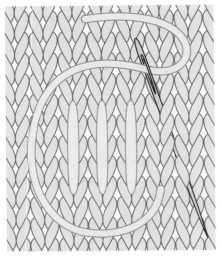

Straight stitch

To make this stitch, simply take the yarn out at the starting point and back down into the work where you want the stitch to end.

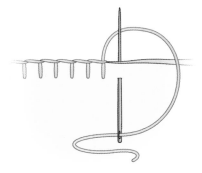

Blanket stitch

Bring the needle through at the edge of the fabric. Push the needle back through the fabric a short distance from the edge and loop the thread under the needle. Pull the thread through to make the first stitch, then make another stitch to the right of this. Continue along the fabric.

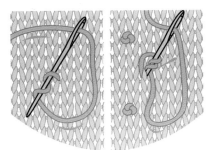

French knots

Bring the yarn out at the starting point, where you want the French knot to sit. Wind the yarn around your needle the required number of times, then take it back into the work, just to the side of the starting point. Then bring your needle out at the point for the next French knot or, if you are working the last or a single knot, to the back of your work. Continue pulling your needle through the work and slide the knot off the needle and onto the knitting.

LINING KNITTED PIECES

1 Press and block the knitted piece, then measure it. Press the lining to make sure there are no creases. Cut out the fabric lining to fit the knitted piece, allowing an extra 1in (2.5cm) around each edge for hems. For example, if the knitted piece measures 11 x 8½in (28 x 21.5cm), cut out a piece of fabric 13 x 10½in (33 x 26.5cm).

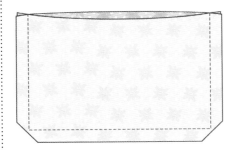

2 Place the two lining pieces with RS together. Pin and sew the side seams, and the bottom seam if there is one, ensuring that the lining is exactly the same measurement, at the sides, as the knitted piece. Trim across the corners. Do not turn RS out.

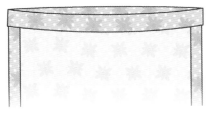

3 Fold the top edge of lining to the outside by 1in (2.5cm) and press in place.